the Cutter

the Cutter

It started as an obsession with hacking hair
from women's heads. It ended with murder.

Michael Litchfield

JOHN BLAKE

Published by John Blake Publishing Ltd,
3 Bramber Court, 2 Bramber Road,
London W14 9PB, England

www.johnblakepublishing.co.uk

www.facebook.com/Johnblakepub   facebook

twitter.com/johnblakepub   twitter

First published in paperback in 2011

ISBN: 978 1 84358 358 5

British Library Cataloguing-in-Publication Data:

A catalogue record for this book is available from the British Library.

Design by www.envydesign.co.uk

Printed and bound by CPI Group (UK), Ltd, Croydon, CR0 4YY

1 3 5 7 9 10 8 6 4 2

Papers used by John Blake Publishing are natural,
recyclable products made from wood grown in sustainable forests.
The manufacturing processes conform to the environmental
regulations of the country of origin.

For those left behind –
innocent victims of fate with an unimaginable
cross to bear for the rest of their lives.

ACKNOWLEDGEMENTS

First and foremost, I owe a debt of gratitude to the unrivalled professionalism of Editor-in-Chief Michelle Signore, whose dedication to detail and eagle-eyed scrutiny underpinned this tricky and highly complex project throughout the entire production process.

My thanks also go to the *Daily Echo*, Bournemouth reporting team, led by Andy Martin, who generously shared information that had been harvested remorselessly over nine years of an international police investigation.

Finally, a big thank you to those investigators, who must remain anonymous, who cheerfully offered guidance, whenever legally and operationally possible.

PUBLISHER'S NOTE

In June 2011, Danilo Restivo was found guilty of the murder of Heather Barnett at Winchester Crown Court. Following the conviction, the CPS issued a statement. The following is an extract from that statement: 'The jury also heard evidence that Danilo Restivo was responsible for the murder of Elisa Claps in Italy. There were striking similarities between the two murders. It is important to say, however, that the jury was not asked to decide whether or not Danilo Restivo murdered Elisa Claps and he awaits his trial in Italy for that.'

CONTENTS

SHATTERED LIVES

Most people feel safe in their homes; Heather Barnett and her two children most certainly did – a fatal mistake for which there would be no second chance.

Heather, at the age of 48, had built up a reputation as a skilled seamstress. Self-employed, there was no shortage of work. People from all over the county of Dorset came to her with sewing jobs – from repairing curtains and shortening trousers to making dresses for weddings and other special occasions. She was a consummate professional with a keen eye for detail and an artistic temperament; a perfectionist in all that she undertook, but especially as a mother.

As you would expect, her home in Capstone Road, Bournemouth, was always tidy and cosy. She had made most of the curtains, cushions, tablecloths and furniture covers – also many of her daughter's clothes. Her children – Terry, aged 14, and Caitlin, three years younger than her brother, though equally mature intellectually – were always smartly turned out; they were Heather's pride and joy. Any patching of their clothes was cleverly camouflaged. The children's friends often asked Heather to mend their frayed jackets or snagged leggings and she always obliged smilingly. Being a caring mother and a friend to her children and their companions was more important to her than anything else.

Most days she would be fielding phone calls incessantly from regular customers and others who had just heard about her services. Increasingly important to her as a single mother, her cottage industry flourished on the most effective form of advertising – word of mouth.

Tuesday, 12 November 2002 dawned overcast and chilly. Bleak winter was in the air, even in Bournemouth, a coastal town renowned for its relatively mild climate. The weekday morning ritual was in full swing by 8.00am in the Barnett household: territorial fights over the bathroom, squabbles over countless petty issues, the usual brother versus sister friction, and breakfast on the run. A peck on the cheek for mum and jaunty waves as Heather dropped off the children at Summerbee School in Mallard Road at just after 8.30am.

'Be careful,' said Heather, as her children scrambled from the car. How ironic that her last words to her children were a caution to them.

Bournemouth was a busy town, with rush-hour gridlock to match any city. Commuters battling against the clock made roads hazardous, especially on a wet morning like that Tuesday. The pavements were scarcely any safer, having been turned into rat-runs by cyclists seeking refuge from aggressively-driven vehicles. A CCTV camera, attached to the Richmond Arms pub in Charminster Road, filmed Heather's white Fiat Punto turning into Capstone Road at 8.37am.

Heather had a daily routine. As soon as her children were at school, she would sit in the kitchen at home with a cup of tea, possibly nibbling a round of toast as she listed her schedule for the day in order of priority. There were costumes to be made for other children's Christmas concerts and school plays; although not desperately urgent, she preferred to keep ahead of the game, if possible, rather than having to play catch-up, which was always stressful. Self-discipline was one of her business strengths.

There was already more than enough stress in her life with the demands of bringing up two children alone on limited resources. Not that Heather was a person to complain. She was more than happy with her lifestyle and considered herself fortunate to have such well-balanced and responsible children. She was optimistic about their future. She talked with motherly pride to friends and neighbours about Terry and Caitlin, especially with reference to their progress at school and how, despite difficult times ahead for job-seekers, she was convinced her children would be trailblazers in whatever careers they chose. In many respects, she was a mum on a mission.

Although the family did not want for anything, Heather, just like any other single parent, needed to keep a watchful eye on the budget. Any sudden, unexpected, sizeable expense was capable of knocking their economy off kilter. Nevertheless, the future looked rosy that November morning, despite the swiftly gathering clouds.

Commissions were coming in and Heather had even

begun to plan for a bumper Christmas. She had already started a provisional list of Christmas presents to buy — mainly for her children. She liked to be organised; it was good for business, demonstrating to customers that she was professional and no dilettante. It also boosted her confidence, making her feel in control of her own destiny — the kind of fool's paradise we all cocoon ourselves in, though few of us, fortunately, pay so dearly for our one-dimensional faith in self-determination.

After breakfast, she took a few phone calls but did not make any. The only call made that day from Heather's landline was at 5.53am that morning. Heather had been an early riser all her adult life and was a great believer in hitting every day on the run. She was very much a morning person, so typical of people born and raised in the country, well away from cities and urban sprawls. 'It's the early bird that catches the worm' was one of her favourite maxims.

Everything in her life was so normal that Tuesday morning. No alarm bells or portent of the seismic events just around the corner. Known by one person only, the countdown towards oblivion had already begun. Without warning, without a chance to take avoiding action, without prior threats, death came cold-calling with a knock on the front door, probably a few minutes before 9.30am.

★ ★ ★

Now fast-forward the clock to mid-afternoon of the same day.

Terry and Caitlin left school shortly after 3.30pm and walked home together as usual. Their mother's car was parked in the drive. Everything appeared routine and normal so far. Their modest but comfortable home was the ground-floor flat and they made their way to the side of the house, where the entrance was situated.

Caitlin tried the door; it was unlocked. She opened it and skipped inside, happy to be home, as always. Another day of school over; always something to be celebrated! Going into the house ahead of her brother was yet another little afternoon ritual, a gesture of old-fashioned respect — ladies first.

As soon as Terry had closed the front door behind him, Caitlin called to her mother, something else she always did on their return from school. There was no answer. Strange, thought Caitlin, especially as the car was outside. Heather always liked to be indoors to greet them with a hug, kisses and eager questions about their day at school. If there was any shopping to be done, she tried to do it in the morning.

Terry thought his mother might be in the garden. However, almost immediately, he was overcome by an uneasy feeling that something was wrong. 'There was a big silence,' he would later tell the police. 'I didn't like it.' The silence was eerie and seemed to engulf and swallow up the pair of them. Unlike the comforting and peaceful silence of a church or cathedral, this was brooding and malevolent.

Terry noticed that the bathroom door was closed. Caitlin knocked on it, saying, 'Mum! Are you in there … Mum?' Silence still. Creepy silence. So she tentatively inched open the door.

Theirs was a home of laughter and fun. A good-to-be-alive home. Whatever was happening outside, within their four walls the sun always shone, even on miserable, damp

November days like this one. Not any more, though. In the next few seconds, everything for those two children was to change for ever.

Terry and Caitlin were far too young, of course, to have seen the classic Alfred Hitchcock movie *Psycho,* but for an older generation the gore that confronted these children would have triggered violent images of Janet Leigh and a bloodbath in a shower.

Heather Barnett had not gone out. She was on the bathroom floor in a pool of blood. Her legs were straight and her left hand rested beside her body. Her right hand had been placed on her lower stomach, a clump of light-brown hair grasped in the palm of her hand. About 30 human hairs, of a different colour to hers, were in her other hand. Her upper clothes had been pulled up to the level of her breasts, while her jeans had been unfastened and pulled down slightly, exposing the top of her pubic hair. Her bra had been snapped at the front between the two cups. Both breasts had been cut off and lay on the floor beside her head. Her throat had been cut ear to ear, the wound gaping to the extent that her spine was exposed. There was also a palpable injury to the top of her head.

Heather's head and shoulders lay in a pool of blood. A trail of this same oozing red liquid led from the workroom, through the lounge, to the bathroom. Further bloodstains and smears were noted on various surfaces at around waist-level, near an upturned stool, adjacent to the patio doors in the workroom.

But the sight the children will remember to their own dying day was that of their mother's butchered breasts. Each one had been sliced off and placed beside Heather's head on the floor.

Seconds later, they were in the street again, this time dashing into the road, running up and down in a daze like headless chickens, flailing their arms, stopping traffic and pedestrians, their screams muted, shock paralysing their vocal cords.

Breaking away from his sister, Terry stumbled back into the flat to make a breathless 999 emergency call, willing his voice not to desert him again. His call was answered almost immediately.

'My mum's just been murdered!' he blurted, his voice strong again, but tortured. He was no fool. He knew there was no life left in his mother and that this carnage was in no way the result of an accident.

The telephone operator tried to calm Terry, who, fearing that he might not be taken seriously, felt it necessary to add, 'This isn't a joke. She *is* dead.'

Trained to deal with these situations, though mercifully they were only rarely of such depravity, the operator knew the importance of keeping the line open for as long as possible, so that all the priority information could be elicited from the caller, simultaneously noting the time that was on her screen.

Often callers caught up in tragic circumstances who are hysterical or panicking can hang up before providing all the necessary information. All 999s are automatically recorded to enable the police later to hear exactly what has been said when a crime or accident was first reported. A caller claiming to have been genuinely panicking, for example, when making a 999 call might be found to lack the ring of truth when played in court months later to a jury. Therefore, operators who field 999 calls are trained to remain calm and logical, but clearly directive in their questioning, in order to elicit essential information as efficiently and as accurately as possible.

Despite the harrowing situation he was caught up in, Terry managed to keep his head while on the phone, but quickly went to pieces afterwards as shock kicked in.

Terry joined his sister in the street, where a couple were just pulling up opposite their house. The woman in the car was Fiamma Marsango, who lived at 93 Capstone Road, and she was accompanied by her future husband, Danilo Restivo, an Italian, who had moved in with her a few months earlier.

Terry beckoned frantically to the woman, pleading with her to come to them. Fiamma wondered what on earth was going on. As another neighbour said, 'When children are running about shouting, "Murder!" it takes some while to compute. It's the last thing in the world you're expecting to hear and you don't, at first, take it seriously. You start looking around for the tell-tale signs of something like *Candid Camera*. Murder comes to other people, to other streets, not your own.'

Restivo went with Fiamma to the children. The staccato, disjointed and muddled narrative, naturally devoid of chronology, that spilled from the children appalled Fiamma. 'You poor children,' she muttered. 'Have you called the police?'

'Yes, yes,' Terry said tearfully.

Sobbing uncontrollably, Caitlin held her head in her hands, the tears dripping on to the road, her entire body shaking in shock.

Restivo put his arms around both children, pulling them into him, hugging them tight.

'Come with us,' said Fiamma. 'Don't go back into your home. Come with us to wait for the police.'

Restivo assured Terry and Caitlin that they would be safe with them. Still with his arms around the children, he guided them into number 93.

Another passer-by who tried to console Heather's children also made a 999 call. By then, however, the emergency services – police and paramedics – were already on their way. Grief-stricken, the children were now inconsolable – shivering, sobbing, muttering incoherently, trying desperately to convince themselves that this was not happening.

Little groups were gathering on both pavements. Most of the people were casually interested, keen to discover the cause of the commotion, and shocked when scant news of the discovery filtered through. They were most concerned for Terry and Caitlin, whose distress had been obvious. And yet none of them was aware at this point of the full horror of the situation and the traumatic sight that had greeted the children. Very sensibly, none of the bystanders had ventured into the house. Natural instinct might have been to rush into the flat to try to administer first-aid and revive Heather, but Terry's graphic account, albeit brief and fragmented, had been sufficiently succinct to ward off any aspiring Good Samaritan. Probably also on their minds was the fear that, if Heather had indeed been brutally murdered, her killer could still be on the premises.

People always complain of the 'agonising wait' for an ambulance and the police, but it is rarely as long as imagined. In life-and-death crises, the perception of time has a tendency to become distorted; similarly here, the reality of time had little meaning for the bystanders or the traumatised children.

'Where are they? They're not coming. No one's coming!' Terry despaired. 'They didn't believe me. They thought I was fooling around. I knew it!'

But the wail of distant sirens soon confirmed that the emergency services were indeed on their way. Still, it seemed 'an age' to those waiting before the fleet of police cars and an ambulance stopped in a squeal of brakes outside the house. And with them, one of the most baffling murder hunts in the history of modern crime was about to begin.

From this moment, police procedure took over. As soon as the first police officers at the house had confirmed that Heather Barnett had been unlawfully killed, the entire road was declared a crime scene and secured. No one would be allowed to contaminate evidence. A police doctor was called out, the coroner's office was informed, and specialist scene-of-crime officers were despatched by the van-load.

The response to a crime of this nature is swift and involves massive manpower and resources. Everything happens fast at first. This is essential because all statistics demonstrate that if a murder is not solved within the first 48 hours, the odds of a successful conclusion diminish proportionately by the day.

Other statistical factors also strongly influence the attitudes and procedures of the police at the outset of any murder investigation. The vast majority of all murders are committed by someone the victims know, maybe even live and share a bed with – a spouse, a lover, a former husband, a jealous work colleague or maybe even an 'ex'. The police cannot ignore these known factors. They are foremost in the thinking of all detectives because they are so often signposts to a swift and tidy conclusion.

So, despite the visual message from the bathroom of Heather Barnett's flat, it was imperative that the police began by following the tried and tested methods of inquiry, and sticking with the conventional route until forced to look elsewhere. As detection methods have advanced, so killers have become increasingly cunning in an effort to keep ahead of the latest scientific breakthroughs. Some killers, for example, try to make their victim appear to have been the random target of a mugger, perhaps killed during a handbag snatch, simply having been in the wrong place at the wrong time. All these possibilities and permutations would have been part of the thinking of detectives who were quickly drafted in to get the macabre 'circus' rolling.

A fine balance had to be struck in handling the two children. They were in extreme shock, and distraught, naturally. What they had just seen would be engraved on their memories for the rest of their lives.

In one sense, the children were now the priority. How they were handled and cared for – in the immediate aftermath of the tragedy and in the days and weeks to come – was of utmost importance. But they had found the body; they may have been the last people to see their mother alive, apart from the killer. Therefore they were vital witnesses. They had to be questioned. Their testimonies would have to be gently tested for flaws and inconsistencies.

Specialists from the police Child Protection Unit were sent for. Intimate questions had to be asked about the domestic situation. Where was their father? Who else lived there? Who, if anyone, was missing? Had Heather Barnett been involved in a dispute recently with neighbours or relatives? With a man or a woman? Had she been threatened? All these harsh questions had to be put to Terry and Caitlin. All murder investigations are time-sensitive and these questions could not be postponed.

Even before hearing the recording of Terry's desperate and shocking 999 call, his exact words had been relayed to the police by the operator, which included the phrase 'My mum has just been murdered.' On arrival, police found that Mrs Barnett was already cold to the touch. Rigor mortis had begun.

Unless there were special climatic factors, rigor mortis would usually begin about thirty minutes to three hours after death. This stiffening process begins with the eyelids, neck and jaw. The route is always the same — top to bottom — and takes between eight to twelve hours to complete. This rigidity continues for about 18 hours and then starts to recede. The 'thawing' process can take up to 12 hours, although it might be considerably quicker. In freezing temperatures, though, rigor mortis frequently never occurs.

Rigor mortis had a firm hold of Heather Barnett's body when the first police officers arrived on the scene, confirming that, in all probability, she had been dead for at least three hours.

Police photographers not only captured for posterity the grisly scene in the bathroom, but also snapped photographs of every room in the flat and also of the scene outside, including that of the little groups of curious onlookers. Arsonists have been known to derive a great deal of gratification from watching a blaze they had started. Equally, certain types of murderers continue to return time and again to the scenes of their crimes. They have been known to attend the funerals of their victims or to visit the graves. So there was always the chance that Heather's killer was out there in the street, pretending to be horrified, wanting to cosset the children, yet all the time secretly thrilled by his achievement. During the next few days, the police would examine all those photographs, looking for anything or anyone who stood out as being odd or out of place – male or female.

The pathologist who went to Heather's flat carried only two instruments – a pen and notebook. Anything else that he and forensic detectives required was provided by the crime-scene manager, the United Kingdom's equivalent to a medical examiner in the USA. The assortment of accoutrements routinely taken to a suspicious death by a crime-scene manager were containers for 'bottling' evidence, swabs for collecting fluid samples, and a thermometer.

Although the cause of death seemed blindingly obvious in this case, it would not be formally recorded until a postmortem examination had been completed. It was not uncommon, for example, for the apparent victim of a fire to be found with a bullet in the head when examined later in the path lab.

Top of the medical agenda here was to try to establish, as accurately as possible, the time of death: the reason for so much initial focus on Terry's phone message. In respect of getting a reliable handle on the time of Heather's death, the police had some useful reference points. The children had left for school at around 8.30am; they were home by 4.00pm. Rigor mortis was taking a firm grip, so 9.30am seemed a rational estimate; a combination of scientific deduction and educated guesswork. This aspect of a murder investigation can never be exact, unless there was an eye-witness to the actual killing – a rare occurrence.

The temperature of the corpse was measured with a rectal thermometer. In a normal environment, such as Heather's flat on a day in early winter, the temperature of her internal organs would be expected to decrease by around 0.8 degrees Centigrade (1.5 degrees Fahrenheit) every hour.

Heather's partially clothed body had been left undisturbed in the position in which she had been found by her children until the gruesome portfolio of pictures had been taken. The next nagging question was where had she actually died? She had ended up in her bathroom, but was that the location where her heart had actually stopped beating? For the investigators, this was another crucial issue.

The 'A' team was assembling by the minute. Some of the country's top specialists in their particular field of criminal investigation were already there. Others, from near and far, would soon be joining the investigation. Later, it would become an international operation, with investigative tendrils reaching out to every corner of the globe. For now, though, these highly trained men and women were ticking boxes, going through the clichéd routine almost by rote, unaware that they were beginning a roller-coaster ride that would test their collective expertise – as well as their stamina – to the limit for the next eight frustrating years.

The pathologist needed to examine Heather's body thoroughly before it was removed. Gravity dictated where the blood would settle after death. If a body was lying on its right side, for example, lividity (a purple-blue hue) would discolour the shoulder, arm, hip and leg on that side. So if the right side of the corpse was bluish, but it was lying to the left, the inference would be that the body had been moved. Bacteria invaded cadavers, endowing them with a greenish tint, but that did not occur until 48 hours afterwards, so obviously this was not something to be expected.

The carnage that November afternoon, coupled with the devastation of two children, who had witnessed the stomach-churning injuries to their mother, reduced veteran officers to tears.

However, one vital piece of evidence – much, much more than a mere crumb of comfort – convinced them that they would soon have the killer in their sights.

Sometimes, at the moment of violent death, the victim would clutch something, possibly a defensive weapon, and it would remain clasped in the hand. This clenched fist around an object after death was known as a 'cadaveric spasm', termed a 'death-grip' by pathologists. This was usually the result of superhuman exertion, fuelled by an adrenalin surge, characteristically when someone was fighting – or running – for their life. This sort of speeded-up rigor mortis was notorious for throwing the time-sequence out of sync. Without all the other factors, this was one element of this case that might have skewed the estimated time of death.

Gripped tightly in Heather's right hand was a small amount of human hair, retained in her grasp by cadaveric spasm. In the last desperate moment of her life, as she fought to save herself, had she wrenched the hair from her attacker's head? Maybe it was that final retaliatory act of hers that had driven her assailant to such acts of inhuman sadism. If so, surely there would be such a surfeit of DNA evidence that the perpetrator would be in the net within days.

That was the mood of the investigators in Capstone Road, Bournemouth, on day one of this investigation. With such a convincing piece of evidence, the smart money was on a swift and brutally efficient manhunt and conviction.

They were wrong, of course. Completely and utterly wrong.

- 2 -

JIGSAW STARTS
TO PUZZLE

Names and addresses were documented of every person gathered on the streets in the vicinity of Heather's home, 112 Capstone Road. Everyone was told that he or she would be interviewed within the next few hours or days. All this information would be fed into the National Criminal Records database. Desk-strapped officers trawled tirelessly through the names of residents in the streets that surrounded Charminster Road, the main thoroughfare that ran through Heather Barnett's neighbourhood. The computer searches would flag up anyone with a criminal record for violence, sexual assault or harassment. The sex offenders register was also checked. Of particular interest would have been anyone from outside the immediate area who was among the sightseers in Capstone Road as the drama unfolded. Nothing immediately leapt out.

With so much blood and mutilation, plus the fistful of hair in Heather's right hand, senior officers of Dorset Police had every reason to be upbeat about an early arrest. They could be forgiven their confidence — not to be confused with complacency — that the crime scene must have been a treasure trove of forensic and DNA opportunities. One senior officer was heard to say to an angry, tearful colleague, 'Don't fret, we'll have this bastard canned by tomorrow.'

Certainly they were all buoyed up by the impetus of the investigation. They had started this enquiry as if in a sprint, and no one at the outset was prepared for the marathon that lay ahead.

Forensic units are trained to be diligent and painstaking. Fiction, especially on the big and small screens, has always peddled the romantic fable that murder cases are cracked by swashbuckling, foul-mouthed, maverick, beer-swilling urban cowboys with scant regard for authority or the rule book. In the real world, however, it has always been the plodders who get their man — or woman. Nowadays, the plodding takes place in forensic laboratories. Microscopes elicit far more meaningful information than any truncheon. Unfortunately, many a cast-iron case has foundered, not because of a lack of evidence but because it has been 'contaminated' due to rushed and sloppy detective work. Hence the meticulous care, right from the outset.

Hair samples were delicately deposited into special forensic 'envelopes', then sealed. Blood went into glass tubes. Clothing was dried before being packaged in separate bags, with great care being taken not to disturb trace materials. The need for drying was to avoid damage and deterioration due to mould, hence the containers into which the materials were fastidiously packed were deliberately not airtight: the contents had to be allowed to 'breathe'. Everything was labelled, timed and dated. The exact location of each discovery had to be included on the labelling and initialled by an inspector supervising the search.

Everything had to be accounted for, and an audit trail had to be developed for each and every item of evidence. There had to be a traceable 'footprint' of all forensic evidence from the crime scene to the court for the trial. The prosecution had to prove that all forensic evidence had been kept secure and in appropriate conditions throughout the entire 'journey' of collection, collation and analysis; in other words, from the flat, to the laboratories, and to the courtroom. Everyone handling the evidence had to be named; all times and dates when it was tested had to be logged.

If the prosecution was not able to satisfy a judge that the forensic evidence could not have been tampered with or substituted, it would be ruled inadmissible. Paper bags were used to store a considerable number of samples because they prevent condensation and bacterial growth. Vials of hairs were placed on official record sheets that were sealed with wax as a means of eliminating the danger of tampering.

Of course, all this forensic activity was spread over a period of weeks and months. Meanwhile, other avenues of the investigation were pursued vigorously.

The three police officers first to arrive at the murder scene found that the front door keys were still in the lock on the inside. The patio door was locked and there was no sign of a forced entry. The paramedics quickly assessed that Heather was well beyond saving. One of the officers escorted the children back to Fiamma's house, where he stayed with them, doing everything possible to stabilise their shock and distress.

Dr Allen Anscombe, a Home Office forensic pathologist, arrived at Heather's flat at 8.45pm on the day of the discovery to examine the body and note all relevant medical and scientific evidence. The postmortem examination, conducted by Dr Anscombe, was performed the following day. As he went about his meticulous work, he recorded his findings on tape, which were later transcribed. His completed report read:

* *Scattered over the top and back of the head were ten separate, full thickness scalp lacerations, being of linear, curved or irregular outline, between 1cm and 4cm in maximum extent, many showing bruising of adjacent scalp tissue. The largest of these lacerations was a gaping, irregular, three-cornered laceration 4 x 2.5cm, centred 10cm above the top of the left ear, which had penetrated through the underlying skull, brain tissue being visible in the depth of this wound.*

  Large, gaping, incised wound completely across the front of her neck, extending from 2cm below her right ear to just below her left earlobe. This wound had cut through all soft tissues of the front of the neck and had cut through into the front of her spine.

  TRUNK: Both breasts had been cut off by means of a knife or other sharp-edged implement. Shallow, interrupted incised wound vertically down the mid-front of her abdomen, 24cm long, with a horizontal, similar incised wound 1.5cm long, joining right mid-part, and a smaller separate, similar wound 3cm long on the lower left abdomen. All these incised wounds were of dry, parchmented appearance, without apparent bleeding from them.

HANDS: She had lacerations and bruises to the backs of her hands, with a fracture to the underlying bone of her left hand.

CONCLUSIONS: The deceased died as a result of brain injuries due to multiple impacts to the head, which also caused scalp lacerations and skull fractures. The pattern of head injury suggested impacts from an implement having a relatively small striking face, but delivering high impact energy, for example, some form of hammer.

The lacerations and associated crust-type fractures to the left-hand were typical of defence injuries, for example interposing her hand as a hammer-blow was delivered to her head. At least ten lacerating blows had been delivered to her head.

The relative lack of bleeding associated with these injuries suggested that these were inflicted after she was already dead.

Heather had fought to defend herself, desperately trying to fend off the ferocious hammer-blows as they rained on her skull. Her slayer had then committed the atrocity of sadistic mutilation after she had died.

Dealing with the time of death for the police, Dr Anscombe stated that the axillary body temperature at 9.05pm on the day of the murder provided evidence that Heather died 'considerably nearer to 8.40am' when she arrived home from taking the children to school, 'than 4.00pm', the approximate time that her body was discovered.

The doctor believed that the attack, including dragging Heather into the bathroom and mutilating her, would have taken only a few minutes.

Geoffrey Robinson, a forensic scientist and expert in the

examination of crime scenes, visited Heather's home before her body was removed. He concluded:

> The blood-spatter in the workroom, adjacent to the patio door, pointed to this being the general area in which Heather Barnett sustained beating injuries to her head.
>
> The location of the spatter indicated that its origin would place Heather Barnett's head close to the floor. In other words, she was not standing upright when she received the blows which caused the spatter.

Based on the location of spatter in that area of the room, Mr Robinson estimated that Heather's head was about three feet from the floor when the hammer-blows crushed into her skull.

> Since the wounds were predominantly towards the back of her head, it is likely that she was generally facing backwards to her attacker and towards the patio door at the time.
>
> Heather Barnett was probably dragged from the attack location, through the workroom, the living room, across the second hallway and into the bathroom. Further injuries were then inflicted upon Heather. The absence of any blood-staining, due to artery damage, suggests that she was dead by the time these injuries were inflicted.
>
> It was likely that once in the bathroom, the fly-zip of Heather Barnett's jeans was unfastened and the material either side of the zip moved to expose the front panel of her knickers. There was evidence that a fabric covered them, possibly a hand, brought into contact with the inside surface of the front panel of those knickers.

Once in the bathroom, a hank of hair was placed in the palm of her right hand as it lay over her abdomen and some of her own head hair was cut. The evidence suggests that the killer then left the bathroom and re-entered the living room, before leaving the premises by the front door (which was at the side of the house, of course).

The action of dragging Heather into the bathroom, after she had sustained bleeding injuries to the top and back of her head, was almost certain to have caused the attacker's upper and lower garments, including footwear, to become stained by dripped and 'contact' blood.

It was also possible, but less certain, that during the beating assault some blood drops would have spattered on to the attacker, possibly on to hands and face, as well as clothing.

Another forensic specialist, Andrew Sweeting, reported, 'From the footwear-mark patterns found in blood in the bathroom, it seems likely that the attacker was wearing footwear in the size-range approximately 9–11.'

Of course, much of this harvesting of forensic evidence was spread over an intense but lengthy period of activity, extending into months.

On the Wednesday, the day after the children returned to their family home, Terry bravely agreed to be interviewed and filmed by video recorder. The interview was conducted compassionately by Helen Davis, a specialist police officer. He repeated the events of the previous day, from the time he and his sister were driven to school by their mother. Still in shock, he had to relive the nightmare.

He described pitifully how his sister had gone 'absolutely ballistic' on entering the bathroom. He said, 'I saw her

[Heather] lying on her back and all the blood, and shouted, "Mum! Mum! Mum!" He had to drag his sister out of the house and into the street, and almost simultaneously saw neighbours Fiamma Marsango and Danilo Restivo getting out of their car. Of Mr Restivo, he said, 'He grabbed me and my sister and we both started crying.'

★ ★ ★

Heather Barnett was born on 29 August 1954 and grew up in Sturminster Newton, a remote region in north Dorset, a rural backwater that for many people, especially those living in the 'progressive' south of the county, seemed to be trapped in a time-warp. Heather's father owned an ironmonger's shop in which Heather, as a girl, regularly helped out for extra pocket-money.

Years later, when an adult, she moved south to Bournemouth, which for those from sleepy, darkest Dorset, was often looked upon as the land of opportunity, where people grew rich. There, Heather embarked on a curtain-making course at a local college.

After getting her diploma, she made a living as a self-employed curtain-maker, working mainly from home. But for a while she did rent a small workshop in Winton, a neighbourhood about half a mile away from her Capstone Road home. She was successful almost from the very beginning and steadily built up a solid client base.

Heather was soon in a relationship with a man called David Marsh, who moved in with her. Marsh was the father of both her children, but they parted when Caitlin was less than two years old.

★ ★ ★

Heather's relatives undertook everything humanly possible to comfort and support Terry and Caitlin. Social Services had a significant input, but the children had suffered the brutal loss of their mother, one who had been so vibrant, and one who had devoted her life to their care and had always been there for them. A huge responsibility rested, therefore, on the shoulders of Social Services and the children's extended families.

Remarkably for that time of day, neighbours had neither seen nor heard anything untoward. One of the first questions the police were anxious to have answered was the means by which the killer entered the premises. There was no sign of a break-in at the front or rear. A forced entry at around 9.00am on a weekday could not possibly have gone unnoticed in such an exposed location. Very quickly they concluded that Heather had opened the door voluntarily to her killer or he had been in possession of a key. This was a starting point. And very soon they were learning from a neighbour that about a week earlier Heather had mentioned that her house keys had gone missing. This had troubled her, apparently, because she did not like the idea that a stranger might be in possession of the key to her front door. The consolation was that there was nothing on the key ring that identified Heather or her address. 'What niggled her most of all was how she came to lose the keys,' said the neighbour. 'She was always so very careful about those kinds of things; careful about everything, in fact. She was annoyed with herself for being careless, but she wasn't too bothered in the end because she couldn't see how anyone with the keys would know which locks they fitted.'

On 20 November, 12 days after the murder, the interior of Heather's flat was subjected to Luminol testing, a technique for uncovering faint traces of blood. Luminol reacts with blood and the chemical reaction causes any normally invisible remnant to emit light for a short time, in the form of a blue luminescence. This enables otherwise invisible blood traces to be observed in conditions of low light and the results can be photographed.

Expert Philip Webster summarised his findings as follows:

The diffuse, fine, latent spray pattern developed on the carpet was confined to an area directly adjacent to the patio door and the sewing desk. Fine spray patterns are usually associated with high-velocity, blunt force trauma. As a general rule, the harder and faster someone is hit with an implement, the finer the spray pattern in blood is produced.

Within the sewing room and the lounge, there was a long contact smear, stretching from the area of the patio door threshold of the hallway to the bathroom. These stripes were consistent with that of a body, which was bleeding, gently being dragged from the sewing room to the bathroom.

There were several footwear marks developed using Luminol in the lounge and sewing room, and there was a visible footwear mark in blood-staining, located on the wooden floorboards in the small hallway, between the bathroom and the lounge. All the footwear marks developed or observed were from a similar type of trainer.

The strongest marks developed or observed were located at the bathroom end of the lounge and in the small hallway. The closer the footwear marks got to the patio door in the sewing room, the weaker the marks developed became and the more fragmentary the footwear impressions became.

This general trend of footwear strength and fragmentation was consistent with the killer's shoes becoming contaminated with blood while in the bathroom. This area was a strong source of floor-based blood. The marks developed were consistent with a person walking towards the patio door in the sewing room. Each mark is made sequentially and consequently each one becomes weaker as some of the blood contaminate is deposited on the carpet.

In the sewing room, several weaker fragmentary footwear marks were developed in Luminol. The marks developed were located from the entrance of the lounge and on to the area adjacent to the sewing table and work desk. The footwear fragments lead in a short trail, continuing from the lounge area and up towards the patio door. Once opposite the work desk, the footwear fragments developed orientate towards the table. It appears that a few steps were taken in the sewing room away from the patio door and they appear to terminate next to the sewing-machine table.

There were no further traces of footwear marks developed in blood within the property. There were no traces of any Luminol development at the threshold of the door leading from the lounge to the hallway.

The hallway leading from the lounge to the main front door developed no footwear marks at all in Luminol. No bloodstains of any type were detected using Luminol on the hallway carpet.

This was significant because if the killer left the flat by the front-door – there was no other way out because the patio door was locked from the inside – and was still wearing bloodstained footwear, Mr Webster would have expected to have seen illuminated Luminol reactions. Bloody footmarks were also conspicuously absent from the area adjacent to the rear patio door. The strange ending of the footwear blood trail in the middle of the flat was to become one of the most baffling features of the investigation for the police.

Further scientific tests later in the investigation would establish that the killer had been wearing distinctive Nike trainers. Along with much else, the footprints were photographed with a digital camera from every conceivable angle, some of the shots delineating the general traction, while others were individual close-ups.

As soon as the photographing was complete, a powder was applied to the coagulated footprints, which could be 'lifted', in a similar way to fingerprints, by fabric smeared with a sticky gel. This job could be achieved equally well with an electrostatic device. Detective Superintendent Phil James, who had taken charge, had the footprint images sent to the Forensic Science Service, a highly-skilled organisation that supports every police force throughout England and Wales. However, it was not until 2007, five years after Heather's murder, that the Footwear Intelligence Technology System (FITS) was introduced. Stored within the FITS system were at least 13,000 images of footwear types for identification purposes. But even before that innovation, the technicians were able to determine definitively that Heather's killer had arrived in distinctive Nike trainers, and had killed and mutilated in that particular brand of footwear. But, bizarrely, they were unable to shed any light on what the perpetrator was wearing on his feet when making his getaway. Here we come to yet another enigmatic feature of this case.

Although the network of crimson footprints made a trail that was childishly easy to follow and record photographically, there was one incomprehensible feature to them – they did not lead to any exit; they simply went in circles; the blood trail in Heather's home ended abruptly in the front room. This made no sense, unless … for Supt James, there seemed only one reasonable answer, a solution that was almost as unthinkable as the crime was unspeakable: the perpetrator had pre-planned all this butchery meticulously to the extent of taking with him a change of clothing.

Certainly most of his clothes, not just his shoes, would have been heavily bloodstained. After such brutal, ritualistic mutilation of his victim, was it possible that he had calmly undressed, put on a change of clothes, bagged everything soaked in Heather's blood and then let himself out into the morning rush hour? Looking around him that bleak day, Supt James believed that *anything* was possible, no matter how sickeningly unlikely.

Working closely with the forensic examiners, Supt James and his hand-picked team, with the help of diagrams, plus some plausible speculation, put together a provisional reconstruction of the last frenetic moments in Heather's life. Without a doubt, she confronted her killer on the front doorstep, which was only a few yards from the well-trodden pavement. The stone wall at the front was low and did not afford privacy, so any caller would have been clearly visible to passers-by or, indeed, residents in a number of houses opposite, should anyone have been looking from their windows at that exact time. Was he just lucky or had he timed his visit to military precision? Maybe Heather was enticed to the door by a demanding knock or the ringing of the doorbell. Conversely, Heather's lost keys could have been in the murderer's hands, and he simply let himself in.

On hearing someone turning the lock and entering, Heather would have headed for the front door, quite possibly imagining that it was one of her children, returning from school to collect something forgotten or because he or she was unwell. However, the latter possibility was unlikely because someone from the school's admin office would have phoned, asking Heather to collect the child. No matter how implausible, the police had to consider every possible scenario.

Supt James believed that Heather realised she was in deadly danger from the moment she came face to face with her killer. Scuff marks and superficial damage to the property revealed that Heather had run for her life through her home, knocking over furniture as, almost certainly in blind panic, she made a last-gasp dash for the patio door at the rear, her only hope of escape, however forlorn. Any other season of the year and those doors might have already been open, but this was the beginning of winter and luck was not on her side.

She got no further before being felled from behind by a blunt instrument, believed to be a hammer, due to the shattering of her skull. The initial blow, delivered with immense ferocity, landed on the rear of her head, splintering the bone. As she was falling, and while crumpled on the carpet, already fatally wounded, a frenzy of blows were rained on her skull, as if her assailant was intent on destroying her entire facial features. Marks on the floor, plus the trail of blood, proved that she had been dragged into the bathroom, where her breasts had been cut off.

The position of her body in the bathroom and the lividity indicated to the pathologist that she had been moved after death. In other words, she had died from the hammer blows. The wounds left by the breast amputations also provided useful clues about the cutting tool. The killer had been in possession of a very sharp knife, maybe even a scalpel. Was he someone in the medical profession? A doctor, a nurse, or even a path lab assistant? Perhaps this wasn't so far-fetched, as most of the Victorian Jack the Ripper theories have revolved around his having had considerable medical knowledge and surgical expertise. But this was only one of many possibilities that the detectives gradually started to consider.

At that early stage, the strands of hair clutched in Heather's right hand still seemed pivotal. If there had been a struggle and she had wrenched hair from her attacker's head, she was also likely to have scratched him, which would mean that there should be skin and blood from the murderer trapped beneath Heather's fingernails, but there was no such evidence visible to the naked eye while she lay in her bathroom — nor when her hands were examined under a microscope on the slab at the morgue. None of her fingernails had been broken ... so whose hair had she been gripping? Certainly not her own, it was soon established in the forensic laboratory. And, much more pertinently, neither did the hair come from the perpetrator — unless the killer had been a woman.

- 3 -

RULES OF ENGAGEMENT

On the Saturday of the first week of the investigation, police officers were still busily conducting house-to-house enquiries in and around Capstone Road. The task of further questioning Danilo Restivo and Fiamma Marsango, who lived opposite the Barnetts, fell to a PC Fraser. One of the first questions focused on Restivo's clothing that he'd been wearing on the day he had returned home in the afternoon to encounter two terrified children frantically waving him and his fiancée down.

Restivo told the constable that he had been wearing a pair of grey Nike trainers. When asked to produce them, he did so readily. As far as PC Fraser was concerned, there was nothing about them worth noting and, after a few more routine questions, he moved on to the next house, thanking the couple for their cooperation.

The following day, a Sunday, Restivo had yet another police visitor, this time DS Browning, who explained that he was collecting DNA samples from all males in the vicinity, especially those who were known to have been in Capstone Road on the day of the murder. The procedure was for elimination purposes, he further explained. The couple consented to having this done, which included providing strands of head hair and fingerprints. Mouth swabs were used to obtain saliva. DS Browning then revisited the subject of footwear. Restivo said that he had given this information to another police officer the previous day, but the Detective Sergeant insisted that he, too, needed to see the Nike trainers.

By now the trainers had been scrubbed and were soaking in bleach in the bath. When asked why the Nikes had been washed since the Saturday, Restivo said that they were dirty and needed 'a good cleaning'. DS Browning immediately took possession of the trainers, something that didn't seem to upset or ruffle the owner in any way.

The trainers were given to forensic scientist Claire Stangoe to examine for blood. There was nothing visible to the naked eye, a fact already recorded by the two police officers who had seen the trainers at Restivo's address. However, it was common for blood to be present without being visible. A chemical called Leuco Crystal Violet (LCV) is often used in such circumstances to disclose any traces of blood, so that is what Ms Stangoe used.

LCV is a colourless liquid that reacts with blood to produce a purple colour. It is very sensitive and, therefore, exposes even the smallest trace of bloodstaining normally invisible to the naked eye under standard light conditions.

The result of the test was positive – a purple colour was detected. However, there was a downside to the experiment. It was not possible for Ms Stangoe to exclude the possibility of some other substance having turned the chemical purple. Scientists were also aware that animal blood could also react positively to this test. Ms Stangoe had to report back with her findings that an LCV purple reaction was 'a strong indication that blood was present, but could not be presented as confirmatory'.

The LCV purple highlights came from the inner sole of both trainers and the inside upper toe area of the right shoe, indicating that traces of blood were present in those areas. Ms Stangoe reported to detectives, 'The distribution of the possible bloodstaining, particularly on areas of the inner sole well within the shoe (covered by the upper) and on the inside upper toe area, would suggest that an item wet with blood was placed into the shoe, rather than that, for example, blood had dripped on to the sole.'

As for how the blood might have landed on the shoes, Ms Stangoe speculated that 'one explanation could be that a person wore the shoes with trace amounts of bloodstaining on his feet.' Another possibility, she said, was that, 'More blood was originally present, but the majority had been removed by washing.'

It had not been possible to obtain a DNA profile from the samples. Bleach (sodium hypochlorite solution) is known to damage DNA and dramatically reduces the chances of originating a profile from samples exposed to the potent chemical cleanser.

★ ★ ★

Restivo's relationship with Fiamma had begun on the Internet, while he had still been in Italy and she was living at 93 Capstone Road. He first visited Bournemouth in March 2002 in order to 'get to know Fiamma in the flesh'. He stayed at her home for two weeks, before returning to Italy, but only briefly. Apparently not happy in his homeland and pining for Fiamma, he returned to Bournemouth on 21 May 2002 to be reunited with his lover, and they started cohabiting at 93 Capstone Road.

One of Restivo's first priorities had been to find employment. He went to the local job centre and was sent on a course at NACRO, a charity that helps young people with developing work skills. The course was designed to improve his English and also to help him master the Internet and all the intricacies of computer functions.

Naturally, like all other men in his neighbourhood, he was questioned specifically about his movements on the morning of 12 November. He told detectives that he left home between 8.10 – 8.20am. He walked into Charminster Road and caught a bus, buying a ticket at 8.44am. He arrived at the NACRO building around 9.00am, where he remained until 3.45pm. He had retained the bus ticket, which he did as a matter of course because they were necessary for him to claim travel expenses from NACRO.

Very evident at this stage was the fact that the initial confidence of a quick arrest had been grossly over-optimistic. Supt James and the entire Dorset Major Crime Investigation Team were stunned by the feedback from Forensics – not a single DNA clue appeared to have been left behind by the murderer. This killer appeared to be a super-efficient pro, which suggested yet another massive conundrum – cool-headedness and this kind of frenzy do not generally sit comfortably together.

The motive was also another tantalising issue. Nothing appeared to have been stolen. Some burglars were known to be violent and to assault occupants unfortunate enough to be on the premises at the time of a break-in, but murder, sadism and mutilation would be highly unusual activities in that kind of crime. Neither, as a breed, were 'ordinary' burglars quite so accomplished at covering their tracks and dealing effectively with the possibility of leaving DNA traces.

To visualise Heather in the role of a stereotypical stalker's target stretched credulity. She was a mumsy, middle-aged brunette, who dressed smartly but modestly. Her face radiated warmth and compassion. Whatever make-up she wore was almost imperceptible. All her clothes were what magazine fashion editors would describe as 'sensible'. She was not a flirt or overtly flamboyant in her style of behaviour. In no way denigrating her, Heather Barnett was extraordinarily ordinary. She wore her hair in a ragged fringe over her forehead and straight at the back. Her life revolved around her children and her work, most definitely in that order. She read a lot, helped the children with their homework, supported charities as much as possible, and was discerning when it came to watching TV. She was true to her country-girl background.

Sturminster Newton, although scarcely more than 30 miles northwest of Bournemouth, was certainly 30 million light years from clubland and the neon dazzle of the county's coastal playgrounds. Traditional values were still very much part and parcel of her approach to life, yet someone had wanted her dead.

Just two weeks into the investigation, Supt James was sufficiently confident to declare publicly, 'This was a very carefully planned killing. There was nothing spur of the moment about it. The killer knew what he was going to do and how he would cover his tracks to establish his alibi. He knew there was a window of opportunity. This was an attack personal to Heather, not the work of a random killer.'

With no apparent motive and a bewildering absence of DNA clues, the team concentrated on the modus operandi (MO). In vain, hundreds of officers searched sewers, gardens, sheds, garages, drainpipes, dustbins, gutterings, chimneys, cellars, lofts, parks and refuse-tips for the blunt-ended 'cudgel' and knife, both of which must have been covered with Heather's blood. Gardens and wasteland were dug up. The inch-by-inch search of this densely-populated, urban neighbourhood continued for months, until every possibility had been explored.

Murder-hunt veterans were well versed in the psychological connection between killer and weapon of choice. Jon E Lewis, in his book *Means to a Kill* (Headline), graphically describes a blunt instrument as 'the weapon of intimacy, of naked fury'. A club in a man's hand could be his imaginary phallus, an outsized substitute for his own insubstantial penis. The wielding of the club might be viewed by the perpetrator as a form of rough sex, gushing blood symbolising ejaculation and orgasm. A hammer, for example, although snub-nosed, is a sister to the knife when deployed for murder. Inevitably, there is close contact between predator and quarry.

The killer can also 'smell' the fear. The killing is so very personal, very different from gunning down someone or using poison, which are known as 'cold killings'. A poisoner does not even have to be present when striking; it is almost murder by proxy. A gun can be fired from a distance, far enough away to avoid seeing the whites of the target's eyes.

The combination of a blunt instrument and knife was associated with sexual frenzy and testosterone release, as in a climax. Such perpetrators were frequently casually labelled by the media as 'sex maniacs', although only a few ever qualified in law as insane; more often than not, they were aggressive perverts who were incapable of controlling their basest urges. A remarkable feature of the case was that Heather suffered bludgeoning from a flurry of blows, and then had had her breasts amputated, an attack that bore all the hallmarks of sexual sadism, and yet she had not been raped. No semen was found, either inside her vaginal cavity, on her body, clothes, living room carpet or bathroom floor.

Despite the frenetic assault, so characteristic of sexual motivation, the killer had resisted raping Heather while she was incapacitated and also when she was dead. The combination of white-hot fury and cold, calculated premeditation did not seem compatible. Everything about this murder was a hotchpotch of incongruities and unexplained discoveries. Heather did not appear to have an enemy in the world. Relatives, neighbours, friends and virtually everyone who had come into contact with her – either on a daily basis or barely more than once or twice – gave statements to the police that amounted to eulogies. The overwhelming testimony was that she just wasn't a woman anyone could possibly dislike, let alone hate. Nothing seemed to add up.

Heather's sister, Denise Le Voir, said, 'Whoever did this

appears to have been very forensically aware. They knew what they were doing and didn't leave anything behind.' Not only friends and relatives, but also the police, were beginning to consider the possibility of a double-act, a duet of assassins. 'It was premeditated,' Mrs Le Voir asserted.

Supt James echoed the feelings of everyone with any knowledge of the case. 'For these two children [Terry and Caitlin] to come home to find their mother this way is horrific. Not only have they been deprived of their mother, but the killer was so callous to allow them to see her this way. This is the sort of thing you'd only expect to see in *The Godfather*.'

This allusion to a Mafia-style 'hit' was not without significance. He reiterated that he was in no doubt that Heather knew her killer and almost certainly opened the front door to him. Detectives reasoned that if this was a hate crime, then the perpetrator would have to be someone currently very emotionally close to Heather or a person from her past who harboured a hugely significant grudge.

Naturally, the task force began focusing on the men in Heather's life. It is purely a procedural method of elimination, no different from a doctor trying to make a diagnosis. The physician will start with the most likely 'suspects' and work methodically towards a denouement by ruling out each contender one by one.

The odds also play an important part in police strategy. The police start with the knowledge from worldwide statistics that most homicides are what could loosely be categorised as 'domestic'.

Heather did not have lovers; she was not cheating on anyone; she was not a habitué of pick-up bars or sleazy pubs.

She had no history of playing one man off against another, of inciting jealousy, or of neglecting her children. Her life had seemed so uncomplicated. Of the hundreds of people the police questioned, not one could name anyone who might have wished to harm her. She had never mentioned being threatened and, despite having lost her house keys and changing the locks to her doors, she was not a woman living in fear, shrinking from shadows, glancing furtively over her shoulder when walking after dark.

Professional hit men do not advertise their services openly. Inevitably, they are creatures of the murky underworld. There was apparently no one in Heather's circle who had ever mixed with the criminal fraternity. Her brother was a teacher. Most of her networking was with professional people. There was not a scrap of evidence that anyone in her life, even on the fringe, had ever associated with those living beyond the law, especially the kind who would have had access to anyone involved in professional hits.

In most instances involving a professional killer, the prime requirement is to lead investigators to believe that an unfortunate accident has taken place, such as someone falling off a balcony or cliff, when, in fact, they have been pushed. Heather Barnett's murder was the complete opposite in MO; it was an extrovert execution, ending in a publicly obscene display. Simultaneously, the challenge to the police was clear — catch me if you can.

When killers are hired, there is always a financial transaction. The currency is cash; never cheques, never plastic, and never transferred electronically. Money has to be withdrawn. Paper trails cannot be hidden. Experts can track money easily from A to B if managed electronically, but the evidence in this case was nonexistent.

Heather's closest friend was Marilyn Philips. They had known one another for years and were true soul mates, kindred spirits. Marilyn made an emotional and tearful appeal for anyone with, 'Any information, however small, however seemingly insignificant, to come forward.' She was convinced that someone must have seen somebody behaving strangely and suspiciously in the vicinity of Heather's home on the morning of 12 November. 'Get in touch with the police,' she pleaded. 'Whoever did this is still out there, loose, and free to do something like this again.' This was a fear for the police, too, of course.

Although Heather was most likely to have been a specific, pre-planned target, there was always the danger that her slayer would get a liking for it and develop into a serial killer. After all, every serial killer was once a novice, a first-timer. And despite all evidence to the contrary − Heather's looks, style, behaviour and outlook − at this stage in the investigation, police came round to thinking that the most likely explanation for Heather's fate was that, for some perverse, possibly obscure, reason, she had become a target for a stalker.

Two years earlier, in 2000, psychologists had divided stalkers into five distinctive groups. Their research had been conducted over several years and the idea was to produce a model or template in chart form that would assist the police in the early recognition of potential 'serial' stalkers, who might escalate to murder if not identified before they were fully entrenched in their severely destructive, antisocial behaviour.

Co-author of the research project, Professor Paul Mullen, of Monash University, Victoria, Australia, argued that the publicity in the media about 'celebrity stalking' had given the public a skewed concept of the phenomenon. Celeb-stalking was only the 'glamorous' tip of the iceberg and, although a disturbing trend and distressing for the target, was not the core issue.

'Most victims are ordinary people,' he said. Their research concluded that eight in every hundred women would be seriously stalked some time in their lives and 20 per cent of all stalkers would resort to violence. Prof Mullen and his researchers identified these five distinctive types of stalkers: 'Intimacy Seekers'; 'Rejects'; 'Incompetent Suitors'; 'The Resentful'; 'The Predatory'.

Forensic psychologists – often portrayed in movies and TV crime series as 'profilers', such as *Cracker* – were collaborating with Supt James, all fully *au fait* with this latest research data. Taken at face value, Heather's murder made less sense than the shooting dead on her doorstep of TV celebrity Jill Dando.

'Intimacy Seekers' fall in love with their targets, rather than hating them. An author may autograph his book 'with love' for one of his readers at a bookshop signing session. The purchaser, already a devout fan of the author, takes literally the 'with love' inscription, choosing to interpret it as an invitation to intimacy. The self-brainwashing is accumulative and inexorably progressive. As the reader works through the book, he or she imagines that the author is reaching out to that person specifically, that there are coded messages and desire for a secret, intimate rendezvous. Bedroom scenes are read as a kind of sexual foreplay between the two of them, author and reader. The stalking begins very quickly. The target is elevated to the status of an idol. No word of criticism will be tolerated against the icon. It becomes a classic, one-sided love affair, but the 'lover' is inflamed with unbridled passion.

Most of those who stalk the famous come into the 'Intimacy Seeker' category, but so too those who are obsessed with, say, a doctor or nurse. A certain smile or a word of kindness may be misconstrued and lead to years of harassment and misery. Professor Mullen warned that stalkers in this group tended to be 'extremely persistent' and usually suffered from major mental disorders.

Typifying 'Intimacy Seekers' was gay body-builder Jonathan Norman, who broke into the home of movie director Steven Spielberg. Norman had fantasised for years about raping Spielberg until he reached a point where virtual reality was no longer sufficient and he had to cross the line. He was gaoled for 25 years.

The victims of 'Rejects' are nearly always former lovers, partners or spouses. They refuse to accept the breakdown of a relationship or the break-up of a marriage, interpreting the situation as a mistake or 'aberration' on the part of their erstwhile domestic partner, and pester for a reconciliation. They will not take no for an answer and will go to unacceptable lengths to try to achieve their goal. The longer they are thwarted, the more they seek revenge, as much as attempting to rekindle the flame of affection, and it is at this point that they become a danger.

An example of a 'Reject' was Nigel Harris, who, in 1999, gained national notoriety as Britain's first convicted e-mail stalker. He bombarded his former lover with as many as eight erotic e-mail messages per hour on her home PC, as well as sticking 'Wanted' posters on windows of her car in a vain bid to win her back. Naturally, this was one of the categories that interested the Dorset investigators, but there was not a scrap of evidence hinting that any man from a distant romantic liaison with Heather had been trying to seduce her back into his arms and bed. No threatening mail, letters, phone calls or graffiti were found – and no complaints from her about being followed or molested.

'Rejects' do not go from rejection to attack in one impulsive leap. They always begin with hard-sell persuasion and immature pleading; bleating, in fact. The route to revengeful aggression is usually a long and circuitous one. So a 'Reject' was another one for the back-burner; not a card to be discarded irrevocably, but one to be kept up the sleeve, just in case something turned up unexpectedly to transform it into an ace.

'Incompetent Suitors' are exactly what the tag implies. They are attracted to someone but lack the social skills and chat-up lines to have any chance of lighting that magical spark that ignites a relationship. Because of their inadequacies, they are often as bad at stalking as connecting with someone. Collectively, they derive little or no satisfaction from harassing the 'object' of their desire. A common trait is that they give up easily, only to fall immediately for another 'love of their life', usually someone they have never exchanged more than a few words with or perhaps have not even met; just a face in the crowd, perhaps. Although commonly of low intellect, they may have a very high opinion of themselves, sometimes believing themselves to be irresistible, and becoming disgruntled and resentful when they are not worshipped appropriately by the opposite sex.

Michael Dale was an example of an 'Incompetent Suitor' who defied the stereotype. As an anaesthetist, he had a high IQ and was an academic high-flyer, but a serial failure when it came to wooing women. He stalked a nurse, aged 23, who worked at the same hospital in Preston, Lancashire. One day he left a note, wedged behind a windscreen-wiper of the nurse's car, to the effect that he would understand if she rated him a 'sad, middle-aged git'. He was fined and a restraining order was imposed, banning him from going within a quarter-of-a-mile of the nurse.

'Resentful Stalkers' feel sorry for themselves, convinced that they have been sinned against. They are the innocent party and are hell-bent on retribution. Their victim could be someone they loathe, but not always; he or she might merely be a symbolic representative of a social class, trade, profession or political party that they happen to despise. These are frequently 'workplace stalkers', who are stimulated and appeased, to some extent, by the fear they generate.

Although those who resort to stalking due to extreme resentment sometimes suffer from paranoia, such as schizophrenia, the majority have 'self-righteous personalities', said Professor Mullen. They are convinced that they have God and virtue in their corner and are morally superior to other people.

Anthony Burstow, a veteran of the Falklands War, was the first person to be gaoled in Britain for causing psychological grievous bodily harm to a woman he had stalked for six years. Sentenced to three years in prison, he was released after fifteen months, only to immediately recommence his reign of terror against the same woman. Such was his obsession and derangement that he even changed his name to that of the woman's last known boyfriend. This was the landmark case that paved the way for the introduction in 1997 of anti-stalking laws.

Finally, the 'Predatory Stalkers' – these are a heartless, malevolent breed and mean business, the equivalent of Great White sharks of the seas, unerringly homing in on their prey until ready to strike. Their stalking is a pernicious prelude to an attack. They are not looking for a relationship, just one-sided violence. To these passionless hunters, it is warfare, building day by day, hour by hour, towards an unprovoked and unanticipated ambush.

With these highly-motivated predators, the stalking is structured along military lines, where information-gathering is an integral ingredient of the preparation. The initial groundwork comprises reconnoitring; finding out as much as possible about the target's habits and daily routine. What time does she rise in the morning … leave for work (by car or public transport) … have lunch … does she eat alone … and how late does she stay at the office, shop, hospital, and so forth? The evening ritual is pivotal: does she date, dine out – if so, where – and, finally, what time to bed? How many people live in the same house? How many silhouettes in the bedroom? In other words, is the target sleeping alone? Everything is memorised, or even written in a special log-book.

When the bedroom light of the target is switched off, this is when the 'Predatory Stalker' at last relaxes for the night; for him, it is equivalent to taking a Valium and quickly coming down from a dizzy 'high'. With the quarry safely tucked up in bed for the night, it is immaterial to him whether she is sleeping alone or with someone else. Here is a fundamental difference from the other stalker groups – jealousy and the impulse for possession are absent; there is no emotional traction. This is a very different blood sport.

There will be numerous dress rehearsals for the 'big event'. Much pleasure is derived from voyeurism and its intrusions. The fantasising over what lies ahead is almost more rewarding to these stalkers than the actual enactment. In fact, the physical assault, which is almost always sexual in nature, can be an anticlimax, tantamount to bringing down the curtain for the last time on a long-running show. Underpinning the jet-propelled single-mindedness is the lust for power and control over another person, a woman seen as helpless. It is a desire even more potent than the one fuelled by tidal waves of testosterone.

Supt James and his psychologist advisers naturally availed themselves of the latest research data from all over the world, and were especially helped by the FBI's Behavioral Science Unit. Supt James and a number of his senior officers flew to New York and Washington for meetings with FBI specialist agents in the field of stalkers and serial killers, because there was much cross-pollination; stalkers so often gravitated into serial killers, with the former spawning the latter.

Many people – particularly senior police officers – remain sceptical about the benefits of psychological profiling in crime detection and prevention. Often it is dismissed as 'wacky' pseudoscience at best or just another gimmick, handy for Hollywood but not much else.

Contrary to popular belief, profiling began in London with Dr Thomas Bond, a police surgeon who performed an autopsy on Mary Kelly, Jack the Ripper's seventh and final victim. Although, as we know, the Ripper was never caught, Dr Bond documented him as daring, physically strong, mentally unstable (rather obvious!) and a quiet loner. No one has ever been in a position to contradict that assessment, but Dr Bond's peers and the police 'Establishment' of the day were impressed, and 'offending profiling' was born.

Modern profiling was taken over in the twentieth century by psychiatrists, who really came into their own in the 1940s and 1950s, when there were 40 bombings in New York City. A profile was provided by a Freudian psychiatrist, Dr James Brussel, suggesting that the bomber was an unmarried man, who lived with a sister or aunt in the State of Connecticut, New Hampshire or Maine, and always wore a double-breasted suit. When George Metesky was arrested in 1957 for the bombings, it was in the State of Connecticut, where he was residing with two unmarried sisters. And he *was* wearing a double-breasted suit. Dr Brussel had also correctly predicted the perpetrator's religion, age and ethnicity. In today's argot, Scotland Yard and the FBI were 'gobsmacked'. The FBI now refers to profiling as 'criminal investigative analysis'.

The police therefore had all sorts of viable theories, but no hard evidence, or a suspect. There was one hope, though – if he was a 'Predatory Stalker', it would have been difficult, virtually impossible, for him to have mounted a long-term surveillance on Heather's home without being observed. The frontage was very exposed to everyone passing; there was no natural cover; front walls and hedges were not high. Capstone Road is no tree-lined, secluded avenue. The only means of keeping watch for long periods, without attracting undue attention, would have been from a stationary vehicle, but parking spaces were always at a premium; no slot could ever be guaranteed, it was a lottery, and that would have compromised anyone who had to be in a particular place at a specific time.

Capstone Road is a relatively quiet, residential thorough-fare, running down from Charminster Road, one of the town's main arteries, which lies in one of the most cosmopolitan and vibrant areas of Bournemouth. There are cafés and restaurants and 24-hour delicatessens, and the student population provides round-the-clock activity. The university campus is no further than a mile away, straddling the border with Poole. Even closer is a plethora of private English language colleges for overseas students, with the diverse smells, sights and sounds of a range of cultures hanging in the air.

Capstone Road, however, is long and straight, quiet and respectable. The hum of traffic can be just heard from Charminster Road, but for the residents here the focus is on their homes, their work and their families. The style here is of middle-class suburbia – good people, caring people, to whom any form of violence or antisocial behaviour is anathema.

And it is this perfectly 'genteel' image that many people still have of Bournemouth and its environs. Indeed, Heather Barnett's violent murder, underpinned by such pitiless sadism and sexual savagery, must have struck people as entirely out of kilter with the sleepy, comfortable image of present-day Bournemouth.

By the 1950s, the pretty, Dorset seaside town had become sneeringly dubbed 'God's waiting room', a genteel resort to which well-heeled retirees migrated to see out the rest of their lives in purpose-built comfort.

The reality is that, by the 1980s, Bournemouth had shaken off its frumpish apparel and upped the tempo of its lifestyle. Nevertheless, reputations, just like first impressions, die hard. Since Victorian times, Bournemouth had been the prim and proper sister in the large − and frequently ugly and vulgar − family of British seaside playgrounds. The sprawling Bournemouth conurbation, embracing the towns of Poole, Christchurch, Broadstone, Highcliffe and New Milton, with a total population not far short of 500,000, was Britain's Miami Beach, a magnet for prosperous pensioners from the north, the Midlands and London.

This picture of octogenarian gentility, however, does not ring true nowadays. In actual fact, Bournemouth had morphed from the United Kingdom's Miami Beach into Los Angeles − a linear, coast-hugging megalopolis, spread over some 20 miles. When outsiders refer to Bournemouth, they tend to be alluding to the whole joined-up ribbon of development that urbanises south-east Dorset and spills over into Hampshire.

The social make-up of the region is also now undeniably diverse. Boscombe, within the borough of Bournemouth, was designated a deprived area. In one undercover raid, the police counted 60 brothels within a single square-mile central zone. Prostitutes touted for trade on the corners of streets in a residential red-light district, shared with the local headquarters of the Freemasons and the Salvation Army.

The Port of Poole became a gateway for the importation of smuggled luxury goods, drugs, booze and desperate people. Between the 15th and 18th centuries, the whole

Dorset Jurassic coastline was a hotbed of piracy, steeped in the legends of the likes of Long John Silver and Blackbeard. By the 1990s, London gangs had been convicted of armed robbery on glitzy jewellers' shops, making speedy getaways along the motorway corridor to the Smoke. In one week, there were four murders. A far cry, then, from the sleepiness of yesteryear.

A university and myriad language schools had turned on its head the prevailing age demographic. In this cosmopolitan melting pot, the nasal sounds of Liverpool, for example, coexisted comfortably with the more melodic dialects of Florence, Madrid and Paris. Historically cemented by wealth, the area as an entity remains super-rich, with the Sandbanks peninsula, Poole's jewel in the crown, the heady, real-estate hot spot of Europe.

Nowadays, however, it is new money that rules the waves. The mansions of Sandbanks, blessed with their own waterfronts and private marinas, are homes to Premiership footballers, pop stars and self-made tycoons.

So while the staid gentility of a bygone era can still be seen in pockets around Bournemouth, a new, altogether more youthful, money-driven and fast-paced way of life has muscled its way in. And it's here to stay.

★ ★ ★

Diligently, working in pairs, officers called at every house in Capstone Road. They took statements; they insisted that people 'rack' their brains and cast their minds back, not just to Tuesday, 12 November, but to the days and weeks leading up to it. Reports came in of people having been seen acting oddly, but not near Heather's home; none of it carried much weight. Descriptions were vague and too sketchy for the purpose of identification. But the boxes had to be ticked, and every avenue had to be explored, in the hope that one apparently insignificant memory or description might yield a case-breaking piece of evidence.

Everyone on the sex offenders register within the county was visited and asked to account for their movements; alibis were checked and double-checked. Ex-cons, with records for violence against women, especially those linked to crimes of a sexual nature, had police officers calling at their homes. Detectives talked with probation officers. Men charged with sex crimes and still awaiting trial, while on bail, were pulled in for questioning.

Experience told Supt James that, overnight, no one became the kind of killer who had ended Heather's life so sadistically. He felt, as every textbook on the subject would agree, that there had to be a stepping-stone progression towards something so barbaric. Accordingly, there was a consensus that the police should work on the theory that this was not the work of a first-timer.

Perhaps the killer was already 'in the system', someone who had been convicted of a lesser sexual offence, or maybe even a person who had been charged, stood trial, and who had been acquitted. A number of 'cold cases' were reviewed, particularly ones in which the alleged perpetrator was a known entity, but where the victim had declined to prosecute. All this computer cross-referencing and online searching, plus the inevitable follow-ups with house-calls, were hugely time-consuming. Weeks stretched into months and all the police had was what they had started with: a battered and disfigured body; bloody footprints made by size 9–10 Nike trainers; and strands of hairs.

Now all hope was pinned on the strands of hair in Heather's hand, something the police had kept secret, hoping they would prove to be the key to unlocking the case. The hair had not come from Heather's head, but from another woman. The only feasible conclusion to be drawn was that the killer had taken the hair from someone else – possibly as a trophy – and planted it on Heather as a chilling, mocking calling-card; taunting the police and turning such abomination into a game. Also, he must have known, in advance, exactly what he would be doing that November morning with the 'souvenir hair'.

A psychological battle had been started that Supt James publicly vowed to win, however long it took and at whatever cost. In essence, he pledged that the police would never surrender and that this case would not be allowed to become 'cold', involving the winding down and shelving of the investigation.

The gloves were well and truly off. This was war.

- 4 -

SOFTLY, SOFTLY ...

At the beginning of December in 2002, traders in Heather's neighbourhood began a collection to raise money to enable Terry and Caitlin to have a mountain of presents that Christmas. Of course, no amount of money would buy them the one and only gift they really craved – the return of their mother.

Heather's murderer had killed more than a single individual; he had destroyed for ever the joy of adolescence and natural maturing within the embrace of a loving mother for these two children. Everyone was doing their best for them; they were showered with gifts. Materially, they did not want for anything. Murders like this one had devastating impacts way beyond the initial victim.

As Caitlin would later say in her victim impact statement

read out in court at Danilo Restivo's trial, 'I used to have nightmares and flashbacks reminding me of the events of the 12 November. I also don't like going into bathrooms. I used to think that someone might be waiting for me. Now I just hold a fear of what's behind the bathroom door. It was several years before I accepted the help of a child psychologist to help me cope with what happened that day.'

Early in the new year of 2003, a £10,000 reward was offered by the Crimestoppers Trust for information leading to the arrest and conviction of Heather's killer. The police, as always, were still keeping a considerable amount of information out of the public domain. For example, it was not until September 2003, ten months after the crime, that detectives released details of the bloody trainer footprints. And not until exactly a year after the murder did the police go public about how Heather's breasts had been cut off and placed by her side.

Some people, understandably, were critical of the police handling of the investigation, particularly about their reticence over certain pivotal issues, such as the footprints and breast amputations. In some quarters, there was a feeling that the killer would have already been caught if large parts of the investigation had been sub-contracted to Scotland Yard. However, much of this criticism stemmed from ignorance.

The truth is that the Dorset Police were playing a very clever game of cat and mouse. They were hoping to tease out the killer from the shadows of his safety zone. The emphasis on the urgency of finding the Nike trainers was an example of this astute psychology. As highlighted in an earlier chapter, they already had in their possession a pair of trainers bearing traces of blood. If Restivo was their man, maybe he could be tempted to believe that he was out of the frame. If the police were genuinely still looking for the killer's trainers, then the inference was that those taken from Restivo had been discounted.

The public statements by the police were couched in such ambiguous language that the killer was invited to be cushioned by complacency. An absence of DNA clues did not translate into a void of vital forensic evidence. Subconsciously, the police were probably steered by the old maxim that it takes a thief to catch a thief. They needed to start thinking like the killer, and force him out into the open, if this investigation were to have a successful ending.

One crucial clue, which the police kept secret, came from a green towel in Heather's home – a green towel on a chair beneath the sewing machine in her workroom, together with a piece of cream-coloured fabric, on which there were bloodstains. DNA profiling indicated that the blood 'could have' come from Heather. There was no DNA from anyone else.

However, the towel was considerably more helpful. Much of one side of the towel was stained with blood; there were smaller amounts on the edge of the reverse side. Laboratory tests established beyond all doubt that this blood had come from Heather.

Saliva was also detected and, like the blood, was submitted for DNA profiling. Although not conclusive, the odds favoured the saliva also having been deposited by Heather. Detective scientists reported back that there was 'no indication' of the presence of DNA from anyone else.

In her report, forensic scientist Claire Stangoe wrote:

The nature, extent and distribution of the bloodstaining on the green towel and the cream fabric indicated that it was very unlikely that all staining on the green towel was the result of contact with the cream fabric.

At least some of the areas of bloodstaining on the towel were not exposed surfaces, indicating that the bloodstaining could not all have been deposited whilst the towel was in this position on the chair. This would suggest that the towel was placed, or fell, on to the chair after it became bloodstained. One possibility is that the towel was placed on the back of the chair and fell on to the seat. Another is that the towel was placed directly on to the seat of the chair.

The towel was in a location away from the main areas of bloodstaining. One possibility was that the towel could have been used by Heather Barnett's killer to wipe blood from his face or hands before leaving the premises by the front door. This possibility becomes much more likely when taken together with the cluster of Luminol footprints beside the work table, which suggest very strongly that he (the killer) changed his clothing beside the work table.

In view of this possibility, attempts were made to detect any DNA that may have been present on the surface of the towel. Tapings were taken from the towel, in order to detect any DNA that may have been present on the towel.

Perhaps surprisingly, it was not until 2008 that the original tapings were examined for possible flakes of skin and the result led to a massive leap forward in the investigation. With so many tests for the most likely presence of DNA evidence, and so much analysis being done by various investigating agencies, it took a while for the police forensic experts to identify the presence of skin flakes, and then eventually deliver their findings.

The skin flakes on the towel came from two people; one set had come from Heather. The other samples had come from the skin of a man. This was a hugely significant finding, but not one that would secure a conviction on its own – after all, DNA matches from saliva or blood carry a probability of anyone else having the same DNA of millions or billions to one. With the skin flakes evidence, the police were advised that, at best, there would be a 57,000:1 chance against someone else matching that DNA profile. And for the CPS, these were not good enough odds to secure a conviction without other compelling evidence.

Claire Stangoe further advised the investigators that it was not possible to determine where on the towel this DNA was originally located, although it is hard to appreciate the pertinence of this. More important was her statement that 'it is also not possible to determine how long the DNA has been on the towel, although washing or repeated use by other people would tend to remove previously deposited DNA loose on the surface'.

Public dismay surrounded the secrecy of the lock of hair in Heather's right hand. The killer obviously intended the police to be mystified by it and knew only too well that it would be forensically analysed. This was clearly intrinsic to the 'game' he was playing. Not only was it a cocky calling-card, an extrovert display of bravado and arrogance, it was also a smokescreen. The police obviously would devote a great deal of time and resources to the clue. The killer would also have known that the hair, not being his or Heather's, would be yet another DNA dead-end, adding further confusion – a malevolent red herring. Valuable detection time would be lost through what, in essence, might turn out to be nothing more than a sideshow.

Only a Jekyll and Hyde character fitted the personality profile. Psychopaths, such as the Yorkshire Ripper and his progenitor, the even more infamous Jack, could apparently lead normal lives by day and then turn bestial slayer by night, and they never chanced venturing into the homes of any of their victims. Like most psychopaths, they murdered randomly. Setting out to kill on a given night was the extent of their premeditation. They were nocturnal opportunists. Their victims were chosen merely because they were available at the appropriate time and, for them, in the wrong place.

For the police, what to make public and what to keep under wraps required a fine balancing act, which was bound to be more subjective than objective. It had to be their call. The media, of course, had a completely different agenda. In cases of this magnitude, the interests of the investigative team and the media will always be incompatible. Coexistence is difficult and these relationships will always become frayed at the edges, until the job is done and dusted, when both sides come together for mutual benefit. In many respects, the police were damned if they did open their books for inspection and damned if they did not. Catch the killer and you are heroes; fail, and you're incompetent.

Supt James could take the flak as well as the accolades, even though there had been very few failures – if any – blemishing his track record. Although prepared to publicise the clump of hair in Heather's hand, Supt James was far more circumspect on the matter of what was being done with it.

The hair, after routine forensic testing, was sent to Dr Stuart Black at Reading University, Berkshire. Dr Black ran the Department of Archaeological and Environmental Services, specialising in the analysis of human remains. Dr Black and his colleagues had for years been developing techniques with hair as a non-invasive and proven means of testing for drugs and alcohol abuse. They could determine through hair samples if a person had ingested medically prescribed drugs, such as antidepressants and tranquillizers, or illegal substances, including heroin, cannabis, cocaine and even steroids.

A procedure known as Stable Isotope Analysis (SIA) had revolutionised the science of criminal forensics. SIA is the identification of an isotopic signature; an isotope is one of two or more forms of an element differing from each other in atomic weight, and in nuclear but not chemical properties. That is the scientific mumbo-jumbo, but to the police, astonishingly, it meant that Dr Black and his technicians could categorically confirm that the 9cm-long strands of hair, representing nine months of growth, revealed that: (i) they came from a woman indigenous to the UK; (ii) the woman had made a trip to the Valencia or Almeria regions of Spain or the Perpignan area of southern France, staying there for up to six days, about eleven weeks before the hair was cut; the woman had visited urban Tampa, Florida, just over a week before losing the hair; (iii) she had changed diets twice in three months.

All of this extraordinarily specific detail came from this one lock of hair. The woman was clearly a globetrotter; did this mean that the killer was someone who lived out of a suitcase? And if so, had he killed in a similar, diabolical fashion before, perhaps abroad? There was only one way to find out. The time had come for the manhunt to go international, which meant involving Interpol.

Just before Christmas 2003, a woman called the investigation team's direct hotline to say that she had vital information about the killing. She was clearly distressed and highly agitated. When the officer fielding the call asked for a name and contact number, she said that she would talk only on the understanding that she was allowed to remain anonymous.

'That's OK,' said the officer. 'In your own time, there's no pressure.'

But at that moment, the caller guessed that their conversation was being electronically recorded and hung up. The call had been made from a public phone box in the Charminster Road area. A police car was instantly despatched to the location of the pay phone but, of course, by the time it arrived, the caller, and all trace of them, had gone.

★ ★ ★

Because of the ritualistic features of the killing, thoughts turned to the possibility of Heather having been some sort of sacrifice by a satanic cult; not a typical crime in urban Britain, but already there was nothing normal about Heather's murder. Furthermore, although Bournemouth, as an entity, was a sophisticated town, the history of the county of Dorset was steeped in witchcraft and Devil-worship. One did not have to travel far north-west of the conurbation sprawl to come upon rural pockets where civilisation had seemingly shed very little light since the Dark Ages.

Just north of Dorchester, the county town of Dorset, looms the Cerne Giant. Almost twice the height of the Colossus of Rhodes, one of the original Seven Wonders of the World, the giant is a chalk carving on a hillside some 500 metres north of the ancient church of Cerne Abbey. He is 55 metres tall and wields a knobbly cudgel, 37 metres long, in his right hand.

Some criminologists were quick to note the comparison with the lock of hair squeezed into Heather's right hand, particularly because of the sexual significance of this towering landmark. In the biblical story of Sampson and Delilah, it was Sampson's hair that, legend had it, endowed him with such superhuman strength. By cutting off his hair, while he slept, Delilah believed she had sapped his strength, a symbolic form of castration, depriving him of his manhood and reducing him psychologically to a eunuch.

In the warped mind of Heather's killer, was there a connection between hair and male virility? Was there some kind of crazed message that made sense only to the murderer? Nothing could be ruled out; nothing ruled in. In terms of motive, the police accepted that anything was possible.

There is contemporary relevance drawn from the history of the Cerne Abbas giant that links directly with grotesque killings, such as that of Heather Barnett. Legend has it that a giant did live in the countryside near where the towns of Bournemouth and Poole are situated. In the 18th century, the Rev John Hutchins, a respected historian, wrote that the marauding giant terrorised hamlets, devouring sheep and babies, before sleeping on the hillside, now named 'Giant Hill' after him. The fable continues that the locals managed to pin him to the ground while he slept one moonless night and slew him, tracing the outline of his body on the hillside to 'commemorate' the exorcism, and a man had cut a lock of hair from a 'fair maiden' companion and placed it in the giant's right hand with the club. It is also quite possible that the overpowering of the giant sparked the storyline for *Gulliver's Travels*.

The great 18th – 19th-century poet and novelist Thomas Hardy maintained there was an even more sinister feature to the folklore; the giant 'threatened to descend upon Cerne and to ravish all the young maidens on a particular night and to kill the young men the next day' – presumably so that, from then onwards, he would have exclusive ravishing-rights to the young maidens.

Throughout the ages, the Cerne Giant has represented sex and violence and the way the two are interlaced, resulting in his being elevated to iconic status by many sadomasochists in the south-west of England and even further afield. Hardy also made reference to the giant feeding on rashers of baby-flesh for breakfast. Perhaps this notion might appear as fantastical and outlandish as our modern-day vampire stories, but it is not a huge leap for the mentally unstable to accept these fables as historical fact.

If the tales of the Cerne Giant were authentic, then the message was that sex and violence had a certain historical credence and, in today's vernacular, separated the men from the boys. At sunset, the giant was reputed to lope down to the River Cerne for a drink and to feast on virgins – a ritual that is parodied today. Young couples walk from the giant, first kissing the tip of its phallus, to the river, where they drink wine, rather than the muddy, polluted river-water, and make love. The virgin element has lost its credibility because many of the couples are regulars; born-again virgins each time, just to keep up the pretence for the thrill of living the folklore.

Heather had grown up a mere 16 miles from Cerne Abbas. The giant was the nearest attraction of note. It was also central to so many of the fables on which children around her were nurtured. One of her erstwhile boyfriends, John Tandy, remembered cycling with her the 32 miles round trip several times in summer for a picnic beside the giant. 'There were so many stories about the giant,' he recalled, 'many of them quite smutty, as you can imagine. When I was younger, we'd always be passing drawings around in class at school of the giant. We'd have competitions among ourselves to see who could come up with the wittiest caption; they'd all be rude, of course, and the rudest would invariably be judged the best.

'Of course, to kids, the giant has always been a joke figure. Kids will always snigger when they pass it. When I was about 14, girls would say things to me like, "I bet you wish you had one to match that!" They'd be referring to the phallus, not the cudgel. It would be meant as a saucy put-down and I must admit that those kinds of remarks did make me blush. But Heather was never like that. She was always very shy and retiring. Down to earth, yes, but never coarse. Sweet and homely is the way I remember her.

'Although we local lads would never have admitted as much, I think there's truth that we lived in the shadow of the Cerne Giant; the men, too. Stupidly, it gave us a sort of inferiority complex.

'While it made me feel inferior as a male, it was also intimidating to young women, like Heather. She was daunted and even embarrassed by the carving when we first ventured there. It was something of an adventure for us kids. It wasn't the sort of thing you expected to see in public in those days. Vicars were always tub-thumping from the pulpit on Sundays about it being the Devil's drawing and the true test of being a Christian was whether we could turn away from it and not look. We used to joke, "Does he mean we ought to turn the other cheek?"

'Of course, Heather had seen many pictures of the giant and she may have been to Cerne with her family but, according to her, never alone with a boy. I was flattered.

'For quite a time that day, she wouldn't even look at the phallus, as if not acknowledging its existence, following the pleas of the clergy. To be honest, though, I'm not sure how religious she was; I think it was more coyness. We walked round and round the giant and took photos from a distance; it was absolutely riveting. He's such a monster, I tell you! Somehow you just get mesmerised by it because it's so dominating and domineering. It's not much of an exaggeration to say that you're soon under its spell. It's very easy to understand how it would be worshipped as a pagan god.

'By mid-afternoon on that first trip of ours, Heather's inhibitions had waned and we ate chunky sandwiches and drank Coke from the bottle, sharing it, before we sat on the phallus. For me, it was something of a challenge to get her to do it, but by now it was a giggle for both of us.

'We local lads firmly believed that your virility was topped up and we were physically empowered by straddling the tip of the phallus. Whatever the truth of that, it certainly worked psychologically; a sort of placebo effect.

'One childless wife took a camp-bed and slept for a fortnight on the phallus. As far as I know, she never did get pregnant, but she lost her husband. He pissed off with another woman while she was sleeping with the giant. And the other woman later gave birth to twins! That's a true story. At the time, we found it hilarious but, on reflection, it's rather sad. You see things differently as you mature.'

Heather's fascination with the Cerne Giant seems to have continued into adult life, but probably no more than out of idle curiosity, something memorable from her childhood, perhaps.

What is known is that she drove at least twice to Cerne Abbas in the six months prior to her death. She was seen walking on the hillside towards the giant, her car parked on the roadside grass verge. She was in ordinary clothes and not dressed for hiking, and she was alone.

Later, she confided to a friend in Bournemouth that she had driven to the Cerne Giant just for 'something to do'; a nostalgic trip down 'memory lane'. The female friend had never seen the Cerne Giant in person and was intrigued about its origins and legend. There was no suggestion that Heather believed in the folklore or was linked with any cult that was involved in pagan worship or fertility rites. She was considered 'far too practical' for any of that 'mumbo-jumbo'.

But one thing she did reveal to her friend was that on the second visit to the Cerne Giant she had felt uneasy there. She was sure that she had been watched from a distant hedgerow, at one moment dazzled by what she recognised as the sun reflected off the lenses of binoculars.

'You certainly wouldn't get me out there after dark,' Heather remarked, shuddering. 'In fact, I don't think I'll ever be going again.' She was right about that.

Witnesses were talking to the police about Heather's daily life in and around Bournemouth. There was no evidence of her having been followed to the Cerne Giant and back to Bournemouth, and the experience had not left her fearful in her home or neighbourhood. While the police were still baffled, they continued to 'keep an open mind' while pursuing all avenues of enquiry.

Indeed, 'all avenues of enquiry' still included even the most outlandish theories, with pagan rituals and macabre, satanic rites being considered as possible motives for the killer. And this wasn't so far-fetched, given the long history of dark arts practiced throughout Britain, and particularly in this area of Dorset.

Witchcraft has been prevalent in the county for centuries. It still thrives, but not just in rural backwaters; the towns have their witches and covens, too. Mostly, the witches will claim to cast spells for people's welfare and general wellbeing. These have traditionally been known as 'white witches', as opposed to practitioners of the dark arts, as in the *Harry Potter* books and movies.

During the 1990s and the first decade of the new millennium, there was a spate of demonic rituals against animals, particularly horses, in Dorset. Many horses – even top show-jumpers and other equine thoroughbreds, having won international rosettes for dressage – were found slaughtered in fields or their horseboxes. Most of the wretched animals had been knifed many times and also badly burned, as if by red-hot pokers. Some had been completely drained of blood. And in numerous cases, witchcraft symbols had been carved into the flesh. The overpowering smell of incense was often in the morning air after the butchery had been performed in stables at night. The animals must have been terrified, going through hell as they were ceremoniously tortured. Yet somehow there had not been sufficient noise to wake the owners, even those who lived next to the stables or fields.

Vets soon discovered that the creatures had been paralysed with injections, rendering all movement impossible, yet not numbing them from pain. On two occasions, hatchets were used to decapitate majestic show-jumpers who were each worth thousands of pounds.

While one could be forgiven thinking that the original *Godfather* movie had been the macabre inspiration for this barbarism, the truth is, perhaps, even more bizarre. These sacrifices had been part of a consistent satanic culture of more people in Dorset and south-west Hampshire than society's leaders would care to admit. Cows and goats had been slaughtered in fields at night; cows' udders had been amputated and laid beside the dead animals; cats had been stolen and killed horrifically. The torture to which they had been subjected sickened the entire community. Often, the dead animals were recovered in isolated spots where there was evidence of black magic ceremonies having taken place.

Although the majority of these obscene and offensive activities, emblematic of sorcery, occurred outside the residential areas, police intelligence pointed to most of the culprits being town dwellers, unlike the stereotype image of the hunched, wizened old crones commuting by broomstick and mixing evil potions in their covens, deep in the forests. These were people who drove out of town in their 4x4s and held down conventional jobs Monday –

Friday, playing the part of ordinary citizens by day and indulging in the unspeakable at night.

Neither was it uncommon for bestiality to be an abhorrent feature of these satanic rites. Some of the animals even bore human teeth-marks, made to resemble incisions mirroring vampire bites.

A short time after Heather's last visit to the Cerne Giant, police were told that she went for a day out to Tarrant Gunville, another rural beauty spot in Dorset with a colourful and infamous history. Tarrant Gunville nestles on the tail of Cranborne Chase, just north of Blandford Forum, a market town a few miles north of Bournemouth, an easy drive and a picturesque one on any day between spring and late autumn.

Over time, more and more people have heard of the dark and unsettling tales associated with Tarrant Gunville, which are so at odds with its noble heritage as a former royal hunting ground. But a vampire legend persists around the place, and proves even now to be a draw to those who feel an affinity with witchcraft and the undead.

The legend starts with the coffin of a William Doggett that was opened during the rebuilding of the village church. Doggett was a steward at Eastbury House, one of the grandest mansions in the land at the time, where kings, princes, dukes and their mistresses chose to enjoy their illicit affairs. Doggett shot himself after stealing from his master and was buried in the church's porch in 1762.

When the coffin was prised open, more than 60 years after his death, the exhumers were petrified by the sight; Doggett was as rosy-cheeked as the day he died and there had been no decomposition of the body. Even more noticeable were the two, bloodstained, vampire-like teeth protruding from his mouth and overlapping his lower lip.

No one has ever explained why, in those austere, God-fearing days, a reprobate who committed suicide should have been on sacred land. Because there is no record of the exhumers having driven a stake through Doggett's heart – the time-honoured method of definitively despatching vampires – the mythology of the undead in those parts has been kept alive. It is good for the tourist trade, after all. The downside, of course, is that it also attracts the mentally unstable and diabolic cults that leave sheep and cattle dead after roistering nights of sex and sadism.

Heather undoubtedly went to Tarrant Gunville as an innocent sightseer, someone who enjoyed seeing landmarks and landscapes of historical note and worth in the spectacular county of her birth and upbringing. Maybe she had been there as a child or as a young woman before marriage; after all, it was only a few miles from where she grew up.

Sooner or later, the police hoped they could start to tighten the noose around the neck of Heather's killer.

- 5 -

EVIDENCE FROM ITALY

Apart from some possible – albeit extremely unlikely – hypotheses, little headway was being made in establishing a motive for Heather's death, or indeed in developing any substantive leads in the case, yet Supt James remained upbeat. 'We shall solve this, however long it takes,' he vowed, with admirable fortitude. One way or another, Heather's killer would be caught, was the message.

Not everyone was so optimistic, though. 'At times, I think we're looking for a ghost or an alien who came off a spaceship, committed murder, and returned, just as mysteriously, to his planet in another galaxy,' said one disconsolate detective. 'This is not an uphill slog, it's a mountain climb.'

Supt James was still pinning his hopes on the strands of

hair in Heather's hand. It wasn't a random feature, he was certain. As the hair did not come from the deceased, meticulous pre-planning must have been involved. More importantly, there had to be a *meaning* to it, or perhaps it was intended as an obscure message to the police; and there was a chance that the significance of that handful of hair had been dominating the perpetrator's life for years, plaguing him even, possibly since childhood.

But whose hair had Heather Barnett been clutching? And how had it been obtained – overtly or surreptitiously? As the theories multiplied, so did the unanswered questions.

One of the most obvious sources of locks of hair was hairdressing salons. Stylists and their customers had daily access to a wide variety of different people's hair. Cuttings would be swept regularly, and anyone in a salon would secretly be able to stash away hair and take it home. This was yet another avenue to be explored, starting with the salon where Heather had been a regular customer for a number of years.

Hairdressers throughout the town were investigated. Profiles were constructed of all those who had the potential to be connected socially with Heather. Every man who had ever been convicted of relatively minor sexual offences in recent years was interviewed. The investigation, under Supt James, continued according to the tried and tested formula. The odds were heavily stacked in favour of the perpetrator having already committed a crime – or crimes – of a violent, sexual nature and he had now 'progressed' to significantly more serious, violent acts.

Members of the investigative team undertaking the background checks on computer databases worked through the names of every person living in the Bournemouth neighbourhoods of Charminster, Winton, Moordown, Queen's Park, Boscombe and Holdenhurst – all areas within a four- or five-mile radius of Heather's home. The tally amounted to thousands of residents. It must have seemed a thankless task to all those officers detailed for this particular chore, day after day, despite being split into round-the-clock shifts over so many months – they were all so far away from the front line and the limelight. They worked away tirelessly and methodically, always hoping – but rarely actually believing – that the next click of the mouse would bring Heather Barnett's sadistic killer into view.

One name that did not appear on any of the UK police's offenders databases suddenly popped up when the search was widened internationally, resulting in a response from Interpol. And the name that appeared on the desktop monitor was not unknown to them.

It wasn't long before detectives from Dorset were booking seats on a flight to Italy.

The destination for the élite Dorset Police 'Flying Squad' was Potenza, a city in southern Italy, squatting among the spectacular Apennine mountains, not far from Naples.

As the capital of Basilicata, east of Salerno, Potenza overlooks a valley through which the Basento River threads steadily, rarely in any great hurry, reflecting the laid-back temperament of this generally hot and dusty region. Like so many towns and cities of Italy, Potenza has a roller-coaster history – conquered by the Romans and made a military colony, it later existed quietly under feudal rule, only to riot later against Spanish domination and then be completely obliterated by a massive earthquake.

After the declaration of a Neapolitan Republic, Potenza was one of the first cities to mutiny against the king. More upheaval followed when it was taken by the French and made the capital of Basilicata. Rocked by yet another mighty earthquake, it was a city seething with resentment. Its people, always rebellious by instinct, launched yet another uprising, just before Garibaldi's revolutionary army brought about the unification of Italy.

Never a place for the quiet life, Potenza was blitzed by Allied air-raids in 1943, with another earthquake exacerbating the devastation from the bombs. Its city wall has survived and at 2,684 feet (819 metres) above sea-level, it enjoys a borderline Mediterranean/Oceanic climate, with a population, at the last official census, of about 90,000.

Another feature of Potenza's culture is probably more important than any of the facts outlined above: because of its long-running conflict with authority for generations and its proximity with Naples, it has always been fertile ground for the growth of 'Camorra', the Mafia of southern Italy. For years, the Camorra had dominated politics, the police and even the Roman Catholic Church. Politicians, law-enforcement agencies and priests have consistently been on the Mafia's payroll for generations in the entire region.

For the rural peasants and the poor folk, the Mafia has long been seen as their instrument of justice, as the only way of getting a fair deal for those who cannot afford fat-cat lawyers.

But when the Dorset Police detachment took off for Italy, they were interested in just one man – and a woman. The woman was Elisa Claps, an unknown quantity to the British police. The man, however, was already very strongly on their radar. His name – Danilo Restivo.

Elisa had been a bubbly 16-year-old. She had long, dark hair, brown, melancholy eyes, teeth fit for a toothpaste advert, a beguiling smile and an impish sense of humour. This girl really loved living. She wore thin-rimmed, designer glasses and sensible-sized, pierced earrings. Like most teenage girls, she did not appear to have a care in the world, except what she should wear. Boys fought over her, though not too seriously. But they did literally queue to date her. One could even go as far as saying that she had a fan club. But beneath her extrovert, public persona, she was very much a family girl.

Elisa had been brought up Italian-style, first and foremost as a devout Christian with all the values that it entailed. Since a baby, she had attended Mass regularly with her parents. At 16, she still recited her prayers when going to bed and when waking in the morning. Her parents were proud of her and considered themselves fortunate to have such a 'kind, considerate, hard-working and very special, darling daughter'.

The Claps family was a very happy one; not rich materially, but buoyed by a wealth of love. What her parents did not know, however, was that their daughter was having clandestine meetings with an older man.

On Saturday, 11 September 1993, Danilo Restivo, who was then living in Potenza, telephoned Elisa sometime between 6.00 – 7.00 in the evening, pressing her for a date. Restivo was 'in love' with the teenager, despite being five years older than her, having apparently revealed his feelings to her two months previously. But it was unrequited love and Elisa rejected Restivo's advances with the bombshell that she was already engaged to another man, whom she planned to marry as soon as possible.

Restivo had not given up, saying he hoped they could remain friends and meet from time to time. Elisa, always thoughtful and never deliberately setting out to hurt people's feelings, had gone along with this proposition. Restivo was to contend later that when he asked to see Elisa on Saturday, 11 September, it had been to give her a present for having done so well in her exams. Elisa agreed to rendezvous with him the following morning at the rear of the Church of the Most Holy Trinity at 11.30am, but she did not confide in her parents.

The Claps family attended the 11.00am Mass on the Sunday, all returning home immediately except for Elisa, who said she was meeting someone briefly, but would be back for lunch, with her friend Eliana De Cillis. After that, the family would all be going on a picnic.

It was a gloriously warm and sunny day, ideal for a lazy afternoon in the spectacular Basilicata countryside. Elisa's parents and older brother Gildo were determined that they should make the most of the good weather before the unsettled days of autumn kicked in.

At around 11.35am, after the service, Eliana spotted another friend, Angelica Abbruzzese, outside the church and they began chatting. Eliana explained to Angelica that she was waiting for Elisa, who had slipped back into the church to have a brief word with Restivo. 'She'll only be about five minutes,' said Eliana.

Eliana waited and waited. Elisa did not come out of the church. Neither did Restivo. Less than three-quarters-of-an-hour later, worshippers began arriving for the next Mass, to be conducted by Father Sabia, who had also presided over the earlier service.

At home, Elisa's mother, Filomena, sighed and shook her head in maternal frustration, muttering to herself in her own dialect about teenagers and their ability to talk, no matter what the time. All this was said lovingly, of course, but with a keen eye on the clock. Everything was packed and prepared for the day in the countryside and they were eager to hit the road.

When an hour had passed and still Elisa had not returned, Filomena lost patience and despatched Gildo to bring her back 'by her hair'!

Gildo hurried to the church, which was empty. The 12.30pm Mass had finished and only a few lingering, elderly couples were about, talking with Father Sabia. He managed to prise Father Sabia away from his depleted flock and quizzed him about Elisa. No, he had not seen Elisa after the earlier Mass. No, she had not been in church for the service that had just ended. No, he had no idea where she might be.

The priest was not the least alarmed. He assumed, like Gildo, that she must have gone off with a friend, losing track of time, forgetting all about their schedule. But the more he thought about this, the more it did not fit. How did she leave the church without seeing Eliana? And why would she leave Eliana, such a close friend, waiting on the church's doorstep for her, especially as Eliana was to have lunch with the family and then go out with them in the afternoon? It was all wrong and totally out of character for Elisa.

In the grip of contrasting emotions, swinging like a pendulum between anger and worry, Gildo asked the priest if it was all right for him to look around the church. 'But of course,' said Father Sabia. 'But I can assure you that she isn't in there.'

Thanking the priest, Gildo hurried into the church and walked up and down the aisles, looking along the rows of pews. He called Elisa's name, his voice echoing. On the way out, he spoke again with Father Sabia, who tried to console Gildo with, 'Your sister must have stopped somewhere on the way home. She is probably there by now. If there is a problem, please don't hesitate to come back. God bless.'

As Gildo jogged home, his faith urged him to believe in the priest. Of course he was worrying needlessly. Of course Elisa would be at home by the time he returned.

But she was not.

And nine years later, when Heather Barnett was murdered, Elisa Claps was still missing. The man with whom Elisa had rendezvoused secretly that Sunday morning behind the church altar was Danilo Restivo, later to live in Bournemouth within a few yards of Heather Barnett.

- 6 -

WHERE ANGELS
FEAR TO TREAD

This is the moment to turn back the clock, back to that Sunday in 1993 when Elisa Claps went to church and was seemingly spirited away.

Of course there was panic and bewilderment in the Claps's household but, at the outset, there was no comparable urgency exhibited by the police. This is not meant as a criticism of the Potenza force – the police in London, New York or Paris would probably have reacted little differently. Elisa, in the eyes of the law, was a grown woman. Furthermore, she was acknowledged to be responsible and most certainly of sound mind. Also, it was not as if she had gone missing after a rave at a nightclub, or had attended a booze- or drug-fuelled party and had last been seen tottering helplessly through the dark streets in the early hours of the morning.

Her 'disappearance' – something of an exaggeration if the police response was gauged accurately – could not possibly have seemed less sinister. Yes, she had not returned home, but that did not make her 'missing'. Yes, she knew that the family was waiting for her prior to the picnic. But inconsiderate behaviour did not amount to the probability of a felony.

True, Elisa was not noted for letting down people and behaving irrationally on the spur of the moment. But she was also a teenager. And teenagers the world over have always had a certain reputation, especially when the heart starts to rule the head.

After a few basic enquiries, the police had learned that there was more in Elisa's life than her family were aware of – and there was nothing extraordinary about that.

People who had been out and about at around the time of Elisa's disappearance were questioned by police. Staff at the rail and coach terminals were shown a photograph of Elisa. One by one, they shook their heads. No one had seen her getting into a car, nor catching a coach or train. Nor could anyone recall seeing her in the streets with a man – or, indeed, a woman. The trail seemed cold before having even started.

All the clergy attached to the Most Holy Trinity Church assisted the best they could. They provided background assistance but, as for the actual 'disappearance', they were as baffled as Elisa's family. Hospitals were contacted. Maybe she'd had an accident on the way home, hurrying, and had fallen, hitting her head and suffering concussion, perhaps even amnesia? A forlorn hope, the police knew, because they would have been the first to be contacted by the medics, but they ticked the box for the sake of the Claps family.

Nothing, of course.

Danilo Restivo has never denied that he was seeing Elisa and readily admitted that he was the man she met behind the altar after Mass that particular Sunday morning. In fact, on that very day when he heard that there was a search under way for Elisa, he came forward voluntarily with an offer to help, just out of church, Christian to the core.

Why had their meting been conducted behind the altar, in the apse, of all places, Restivo naturally had been asked in one of the first questions? His answer would not have pleased Filomena Claps, but was most probably fully understood by the police. 'Because her mother wouldn't have approved. Because none of them [the Claps family] would have been sympathetic. They would have rounded on me. They would have pressured her to stop seeing me, even though there wasn't anything in it. You know, nothing romantic. They would have made her life hell. It was already hell for her. She was having a bad time of it.'

The actual reason given for the furtive meeting had still not been answered. 'She had to tell me that we couldn't be together that day; that she had to go out with her parents. I was disappointed. So was she.'

'Were you angry?' he was asked.

'Not with Elisa,' he replied. 'If I was angry, it was with her parents, but I don't think anger came into it. I was downbeat. We get along so well. But she is very mixed up; messed up. She has a lot of troubles. She has told me a lot and I'm sort of her confidant. Like our priest, I'm sworn to secrecy. I shall never betray her trust in me.'

According to Restivo, the couple had been together in the apse for a maximum of ten minutes, by which time the church had emptied. They had then left separately, avoiding the main entrance.

'Did she seem distressed?' the questioning continued.

'No,' he said, 'just a little sad.'

'Why *sad*?'

'Because she was having to go somewhere she didn't want to. And with people she didn't want to be with.'

'You mean she'd have preferred to be with you?'

'Yes.'

'Did she actually say that?'

'Yes.'

'Have you any idea where she might have gone?'

'No.'

'You haven't seen her since you parted in the church?'

'No.'

'Has she any friends she might have gone to?'

'I don't know of any.'

'Are you worried about her, Mr Restivo?'

'No, she'll turn up.'

'She is only 16.'

'She's quite mature. She can look after herself – better than her parents look after her.'

Restivo was 21 at the time.

While the Potenza police were carrying out routine enquiries to establish if Elisa might have been admitted to a hospital, they stumbled across a fact that not only surprised them but changed their attitude towards the case. Elisa had not been treated in hospital that Sunday, but Restivo *had*. He had had a cut to his left hand that had required stitching. He claimed that the injury had been caused when he fell while crossing a building site, a place he claimed to have taken another girl, Paola Santarsiere, three days before Elisa's disappearance.

Paola was later to deny to the police that she had even been to a building site with Restivo, but she did provide them with some very interesting information. Restivo had boasted to her that he had keys to the Most Holy Trinity Church and that he knew 'every nook and cranny'.

The doctor who treated Restivo at the A&E department of the local hospital was Michele Albano. He said that he treated Restivo at about 1.30pm on the Sunday. The wound was small, about 1cm deep and 1 – 1.5 cm long; a clean cut, not bleeding, on the back of his hand between thumb and index finger.

Restivo was pulled in for a more intensive interrogation. He fiercely denied being Elisa's lover. 'We're just friends,' he claimed. 'I'm trying to help her.'

'In what way?' he was quizzed.

'She's not happy at home,' he said.

'That's not what we hear,' said the police inquisitor, confused.

'There are two sides to every story,' Restivo countered. 'Of course her family would say that she's happy, but that's not what she tells me, which is the opposite. In fact, she wants to run away from them.'

'She told you that?'

'Yes, she did – her very own words ... hand on heart.'

'And what did you say?'

'I told her not to be so stupid ... that she'd never survive on the streets ... that she'd have to do the worst possible things to get money for food and clothes. I warned she'd either end up dead, in a clinic for addicts, or in an asylum. I was trying to scare her out of doing something she'd live to regret – perhaps for ever.'

'Where did she plan to go?'

'Naples.'

'Why Naples?'

'You know why Naples,' he said. 'It's such a big attraction to a young girl. I tried to warn her just how dangerous Naples could be, especially for an unescorted young woman without money. She'd be eaten alive … I said as much. But she's determined … very strong-willed.'

'You talk of her running away, yet she parted from you after only ten minutes because she was going into the country with the very people you say she was eager to flee from.'

'She had to go. She is afraid of them. She has to do things against her will. That's the problem. She doesn't have a life of her own.'

'Yet you also say she's strong-willed. Aren't you arguing against yourself?'

'Nothing is black and white,' he said.

'So she wasn't planning to run away just yet?'

'I don't think so. I thought I'd made her think twice. But you can never tell with Elisa because she can be so impulsive.'

'So you haven't seen her since you were in church with her?'

'No. I don't understand.'

'What don't you understand?'

'Why all these questions? I thought she'd be with her family.'

'She didn't arrive home … that's the problem.'

'I'm sorry. But I can't help you. I don't know anything.'

'Aren't you worried?'

'Not really. She'll turn up, I'm sure. She's just taken off, that's all.'

'Where to, do you suppose?'

'I've no idea. Anywhere to be away from her family, I guess.'

The police believed that Restivo knew far more than he was letting on. Asked for an explanation of what occurred at the church that Sunday, Restivo admitted that he 'led her behind the altar', adding, 'I do not know if it is called the rectory, where the organ is.' He was eager to ask her about her exam results and her studies, and to chat with her about Paola Santarsiere, whom he liked.

Restivo then alleged that 'a young guy' had harassed her earlier that morning before they met in church, making her nervous.

When questioned about how long they were together in church, he answered that they had parted at 11.50am. 'I saw her leave the church,' he said. After she had gone, Restivo stayed to pray a while. He left the church at noon, heading straight towards the building site, where he injured himself.

The Italian police already had considerable knowledge of Restivo. They knew that he had previously taken two girls, Nunzia Mauro and Uberta Corona, to a small room at the top of the church. They put this to him and he made no denial. They also accused him of having Nunzia leave so that he could be alone with Uberta. 'That is not true,' he replied.

Asked if he had kissed Elisa before they parted, he became agitated, exclaiming, '*Kissed her!* Why do you ask that?'

'Because we need to know,' he was told.

'Of course I didn't kiss her,' he insisted. 'I've told you, we are just friends. We like to talk. She has troubles, I could tell. Talking often helps to make things clearer in your head.'

When he was then asked more about his damaged hand, he began changing his story. It could have happened when he knocked it on something 'rough and jagged', he said.

'In the church, perhaps?' the officer pressed.

'Yes, in the church.'

'Where exactly?'

'Well, there's some unfinished work at the back, inside.'

'But earlier you said you stumbled on a building site.'

'I did and that's when I noticed my hand.'

'It didn't hurt you before then?'

Restivo was further questioned on whether there had been any 'sexual intimacy' between him and Elisa. He repeated that he had not kissed Elisa in church – or outside of it – that Sunday. He was reminded that this last question had not been specifically about 'kissing', but more.

Having achieved little clarity over the actual events surrounding Elisa's disappearance, but having little reason to hold Restivo any longer, the police investigators released him.

By nightfall, Filomena Claps was hysterical. Gildo organised a search-party, comprising the entire extended family, all his friends and those of Elisa, and many people who worshipped regularly at the Most Holy Trinity Church, which dominates the town's central square.

Filomena, with Gildo's arms around her, was further questioned by the police. They had to put to her some of the accusations made by Restivo. She was as outraged as she was hurt.

'How could he say such things?' she wailed. 'Who is this man? What does he want? What is he trying to do to us? Has he been turning Elisa against us?'

Of course, these were questions to which the police did not have answers.

Gildo was more composed and forthright. 'He's a liar,' he said. 'Don't believe a word of it. Ask anyone. Ask Elisa's school friends. Speak to anyone who knows her. You won't hear a word against her family.'

And the police did not. Everything seemed exactly as the Claps family claimed. Yet Elisa remained missing.

On that same Sunday evening, Filomena returned to the church, knelt in prayer, lit a candle and wept, consoled by her friends and immediate family. And while Filomena couldn't help fearing the worst, her son tried to reassure her that all would be well.

'She will be found, you'll see,' said Gildo. 'There will be a simple explanation. We'll be laughing about this in a few days.'

Filomena was not comforted by her son and Gildo was not really sure if he believed himself, he was to confess later.

Initial formalities complete, Elisa was posted officially as a missing person. Her photograph, name and physical features were circulated among all the regional and city police departments, especially Naples, in view of Restivo's statement.

'She has not gone to Naples,' Elisa's mother told the police. 'She would never go to Naples, not alone. She's only too well aware of the dangers of Naples. In any case, she doesn't have the money. Where would she live? How would she get by?'

The thought of how runaway girls did 'get by' in Naples horrified Filomena. Naples had a vice trade to match any in Europe for depravity. There was a flourishing market in child prostitutes. 'Virgins for sale' was a common strap-line on business cards squeezed into the hands of tourists. Young girls were routinely sold to North Africa and into Middle Eastern harems. Brothels abounded, catering for every conceivable obscenity. Orphan boys and girls were recruited into pickpocket gangs. And behind nearly all the rackets was the Camorra, Naples' Mafia.

Filomena Claps had a host of very good reasons why she did not want to believe that her daughter had ended up in Naples.

But it might have been preferable to the alternative.

– 7 –

FAMILY TIES

Restivo was known to have powerful allies. His father was a prominent member of Potenza high society and much respected by the town's leading denizens. Apart from Restivo, the police also had to consider the possibility of involvement by a criminal organisation.

To appreciate how the hunt for a missing schoolgirl could be hindered by the criminal fraternity, it is essential to understand the influence that organised crime has on daily life in southern Italy. There is a saying in Italy that the Pope's blessing is second in importance only to that of the Mafia. As blasphemous as that may be, it is not without a certain credence.

The Italian and Sicilian authorities want the world to believe that they have broken the back of the Mafia and that it is a spent force, nothing more than something sinisterly romantic for the movies and museums. Believe that propaganda at your peril; it is the PR of countries whose lifeblood in the new European economy is tourism. The atrocities of 9/11 scared away the tourists in their millions from New York for a decade; London fared almost as badly in the aftermath of 7/7 and, years earlier, the entire UK suffered from the sabotage of Pan Am flight 103 over Lockerbie in December 1998, a mass murder that deterred many Americans from flying to Britain.

Crime in Rome and Italy's northern cities was little different from that of their counterparts in other Western countries; it was ever-present but random, disparate. But in Naples and the smaller towns of southern Italy, including the rural areas, organised crime impacted on everyday life; from buying bread to drinking wine, the Men in Suits took their cut and set the rules. There were two layers of government – the official and the unofficial. Through hard and very harsh lessons over centuries, the general public had come to fear and obey the latter, while not respecting either.

Although primarily Naples-based, the Camorra's tentacles reach into every nook and cranny of southern Italy and for years has left an indelible footprint on the USA crime scene. The semantics over whether the Camorra and the Mafia are one and the same is purely academic – the job description of the two organisations is identical: they murder, they kidnap and demand ransoms, they blackmail, they traffic illegal drugs, smuggle desperate people, trade in slave labour, run the world's largest counterfeiting scams, control toxic waste disposal, groom and manage prostitutes, sell weapons – including nuclear – to rogue states, monopolise loan-sharking, launder ill-gotten money through their gaming outlets, and bribe politicians and law-enforcement agencies.

The Camorra has always operated separately from the Sicilian Mafia, although their activities overlap, often bloodily. In the USA, the Mafia has become Americanised, although a Sicilian import. Now the American Cosa Nostra (Mafia) and the Sicilian and Italian gangsters are as much at war with one another as with the authorities.

The Camorra, like the Sicilian Mafia, is as conservative and traditionalist as any reactionary political party. It is wary of change. Orderliness and discipline are the overriding priorities of such organisations, so anything that might disrupt those principles is actively sought out and eradicated.

In the 1980s, there was an attempt to unify all the Camorra families into the Nuova Camorra Organizzata (NCO). In one region, it had total control of all meat and fish industries, the supply and distribution of coffee, and owned 2,500 of one city's bakeries. And if a prostitute tried to go solo, trespassing on a patch worked by girls from the Camorra stable, then a 'soldier' would be detailed to disfigure her – frequently by chopping off her nipples.

There was a spate of drive-by shootings and the number of clans had soared from 26 to 120 by 2010. Camorra 'soldiers' committed 12 murders in one 10-day period. The following year, there were 120 slayings by the clans. Beatings and disfigurements ran into thousands. 'Unfriendly' mayors and 'hostile' law enforcement officers were top targets.

This is the point – if the Camorra said, 'Lay off, turn a blind eye,' you had to be a very brave or foolhardy individual to defy such an edict, especially back in the 1990s. To a large population of southern Italy, most especially in and around Naples, the word of the Camorra was law. The Camorra was the unofficial government, the chief law enforcement agency, the military ... the Camorra was king. That kind of historical entrenchment is not changed with a few inspirational words of bold intent. Defeating the Camorra would be no easier than winning the war against the Taliban in Afghanistan or Al-Qaeda worldwide.

One man who knew more about the Mafia profile than anybody was Leonardo Messina, a descendant of a family whose Men of Honour went back seven generations. Giving evidence to the Anti-Mafia Commission, he said, 'The people you call "Camorristi" belong to the Cosa Nostra. The summit of the Camorra is Cosa Nostra ...'

This testimony was supported by Tommaso Buscetta, one of the first Mafia defectors to defy the sworn blood-oath of *omerta*. 'Forget about the Camorra ...' he told the Commission. 'They don't exist. The Mafia exists. Cosa Nostra exists.'

The Camorra clans undoubtedly disagreed, but there was no disputing the criminal interplay. Messina had been second-in-command to the boss who ranked next in power only to the most fearsome '*capo di tutti capi*' (boss of all bosses) to rule Sicily's Cosa Nostra for almost a century.

Restivo was a resident of Potenza at the time of Elisa Claps's disappearance, he was born in the Sicilian town of Erice, right in the heartland of Mafia country. Erice, a walled town built on the side of a mountain overlooking the Tyrrhenian coast to the west of the gangsters' paradise, boasts two castles and narrow, stone streets. Except in summer, it is perpetually shrouded in fog, provoking a ghostly feel, reminiscent of

Victorian London and the alleys of Whitechapel, the haunts of Jack the Ripper.

Although Erice is often characterised as being locked in a Middle Ages time-warp, its history actually goes back much further. There is a temple to a Phoenicean fertility goddess and even Hercules is associated with ancient Erice, of relevance when trying to understand its male population. All men born in Erice are reared to believe in their Herculean heritage and inherent dominant nature, to which all women should be deferential, if not submissive.

Restivo, unmarried then of course, and apparently not living with anyone, was again asked to account for his movements on the Sunday that Elisa vanished.

'I spent all afternoon walking through the town,' he said.

'Where specifically?' he was asked.

'Oh, all over,' he replied.

'Did you stop for a drink, for a coffee?'

'I might have done,' he said vaguely. 'I really can't remember.'

'You must be able to remember if you went into a café; it was only a couple of days ago,' the officer remonstrated with him.

'I was just wandering, killing time.'

'Before what?' he was asked.

'Before catching a bus to Naples.'

This interested the police that he should have been leaving town for Naples. Had he gone to Naples?

Yes, he said that he had. He had things to do there, people to see and arrangements to be made about sitting an exam. He was contemplating a career in dentistry.

Naturally, he was asked to provide the names of people who would be able to verify his movements that Sunday. He declined, emphasising that he did not want to involve other people in his problems. He would be embarrassed, he said, for people who knew him to become aware that there was a police investigation to which he was central, albeit as an innocent party. 'It would look bad for me,' he explained.

'Why?' he was asked.

'Because people would think the worst,' he replied. 'People always do. It's human nature.'

His story of catching a bus to Naples seemed to check out. The driver remembered him. Other passengers were asked to come forward. None did.

The main focus of the police was finding Elisa, but there was still no evidence of a crime having been committed. So when the Potenza police quizzed bus drivers and passengers who travelled the Naples route, they were really trying to establish if Elisa had been with Restivo. Showing a photograph of Elisa, the police asked, 'Have you seen this young woman? Do you recall seeing her with this man?'

In the aftermath of Sunday, 12 September, it seemed that Elisa Claps had become a runaway. The unknown quantity, in the view of the police, was over the extent and nature of Restivo's role. Had he helped her to leave home? Had he given her money? Did he know where she had gone? Were they lovers, despite Restivo's denial? Had they rented a secret meeting place or apartment together? Did they ride the bus together to Naples or maybe they went separately to reduce the chance of their being remembered? Was Elisa staying with mutual friends in Naples until Restivo joined her? Were they planning to elope together, perhaps making their way into another country? Did Elisa have a passport and, if so, did she have it with her?

Elisa's mother was adamant that her daughter had not taken anything with her to the church; no change of clothes, only small change lire for the offertory, no baggage of any kind, and certainly no passport. None of Elisa's belongings was missing from her room.

'She has not gone anywhere of her own free will,' Gildo insisted. 'Wherever she is, she's been taken by force. We shall never rest until we have her home.'

During that period, strange reports were being logged by the police all over the province of Basilicata, building up a picture of apparently inconsequential incidents that no one imagined at the time could possibly have anything to do with Elisa Claps.

The police took down the details, but knew that there was little they could do. And to be fair, the trivial nature of these 'crimes' was almost laughable — women were complaining of having had their hair clipped from behind by a stranger while travelling on public transport.

After all, it's hardly life or death, is it?

- 8 -

THE VANISHING

The fundamental mistake, not realised until years later, was for the Potenza police to invest their time and energy in trying to pick up a scent of Elisa Claps from the moment she must have left the Most Holy Trinity Church in the town's bustling main square, the focal point of local social, commercial and religious interests.

If people leave home voluntarily, there is always a trail that can be followed by professional tracers. It is extremely difficult simply to vanish into the ether without leaving a trail of some sort. There are so many different footprints to be followed: debit or credit card transactions; cash withdrawals from ATMs; payments by cheque; calls via mobile phones; and literally millions of daily CCTV images as we go about our lives, oblivious to surveillance cameras as we shop, queue for buses, hail cabs, catch trains or planes, or simply stroll through a park or plaza towards a café, hand-in-hand with a loved one.

Modern life has become one, long, global documentary – reality TV for those with a licence to snoop, from the police to councils and government departments. In today's cities, it is hard to move more than 100 metres without catching the eye of at least one CCTV lens.

Within a few days of Sunday, 12 September 1993, the obvious question for Potenza police and the Claps family was: if Elisa has run away, how is she surviving? Of course, as far as Filomena Claps was concerned, the concept of Elisa simply taking off was unthinkable.

'Elisa hasn't gone anywhere voluntarily,' Elisa's sister-in-law, Irena Nardiello, stated categorically. 'Wherever she is, it is against her will.'

The possibility of Elisa being held prisoner somewhere, perhaps even being shipped out of the country by the Camorra, who regularly sold young 'virgins' into prostitution and other forms of sexual slavery, figured prominently in the Claps's fear, although for the routine-obsessed Potenza police, this was a little too far-fetched to be taken seriously.

However, speculation was one thing, hard evidence was something else – and was the only currency of any legitimacy to the investigators.

Posters bearing a beautiful, smiling photo of Elisa were plastered all over town. Appeals were made on local radio, TV and in the regional newspapers. Daily special prayers were said in all Potenza churches. Filomena attended Mass daily with members of the family. More candles were lit.

Rosaries were worked round the clock. Gildo embarked on countless treks to Naples, frequenting neighbourhoods of the seething city he would normally have avoided at all costs. In every bar and on every street corner, he showed people a photo of Elisa. Every response was identical – a shake of the head, followed by 'Sorry.'

The investigating officers searched Restivo's residence. They found not a single item to link him with Elisa. Certainly she was not staying there. Not a single possession of hers was on the premises, and there was no sign of bloodstains, a fight or damage to property. Neighbours were interviewed, and they described a strange loner who seemed to 'come and go' at all hours. No one had ever seen Elisa with him there; he was not one for entertaining. Women had visited a few times, but no one had taken much notice. There had never been any noise from his place to complain about – no loud music, riotous parties or arguments.

A couple of detectives watched Restivo for a few days, tailing him wherever he went, but when it became obvious that he was not in contact with Elisa, they were assigned to other duties.

Meanwhile, various police departments in the region were sifting through complaints filed with them by women whose hair had been clipped in public. Of course, there was no reason for these incidents to be cross-referenced with the Elisa Claps case. For a start, they were given a much lower priority. Indeed, many of the women 'victims' were semi-amused by their experience.

'I couldn't believe it,' said one incredulous newlywed. 'There I was, sitting on the bus, reading a magazine, and I felt as if a few strands of my hair at the back were being touched and played with. Then I heard a snipping sound. Just the one snip. I turned my head sideways and saw some loose hairs on my shoulder. They looked like mine and I swung right round. A young guy was sitting behind me, staring out of the window, hands in pockets, as if he'd no idea what was going on. "Did you just cut my hair?" I said.

'"Me?" he said, all innocent-like. "What are you talking about?"

'I didn't know what was going on. "You just messed with my hair," I said.

'"You're crazy," he said.

'I got off the bus at the next stop, even though I was going further. He freaked me out. When I got indoors, I went straight to my bedroom and examined the back of my head with a hand-held mirror and the dressing-table mirror. To my astonishment, a whole chunk of hair had been cut away.'

This was a statement made to the police in Naples by a woman aged 23 who worked as a secretary. According to this woman, who spoke to a reporter on her local community newspaper, the police more or less asked her, 'So what do you expect us to do?'

'I think they thought it was funny, a bit of a joke,' she said. The police had asked her if she knew the man.

'Never seen him before,' she had replied.

'So he's not an ex-boyfriend?' she was asked.

'If he had been, I'd have clawed out his eyes,' she had answered.

Her feistiness had ebbed, however, when asked for a description of her molester. 'Youngish, ordinary, wearing sunglasses,' she said. 'I didn't get much of a look at him.'

This answer did not, apparently, much impress the interviewing officer because he wrote an exclamation mark in a side-column on his report sheet, next to the witness's comment. He also wrote, 'Yet he was sitting right behind her and she turned to face him!'

The witness concluded her statement: 'He kept looking out the window most of the time, even when I was talking to him. I wanted to get away from him as quickly as possible.'

When asked if she would be able to identify him in a line-up or from a rogues' gallery photograph, she replied, 'I couldn't honestly say.'

She spent an hour thumbing through mug shots of convicted, small-time sex-pests, but it proved a fruitless exercise.

The report went into a folder and into the bottom drawer in a filing cabinet ... to gather dust.

* * *

There were incidents reported in Rome, Milan and Turin of women having their locks shorn from behind by a stranger while using public transport. Unknown to the Italian police, similar allegations were being made in Madrid, Malaga and Paris; also in the South American countries of Brazil, Peru and Venezuela, plus the North American cities of Miami and New Orleans. But there was no big picture; that was the problem, the critical linking of apparently random events into a meaningful pattern. There was no joined-up reporting, no worldwide cohesion between law enforcement agencies. Each complaint was treated as a one-off. There was no cross-matching and nonexistent collaboration – not even in Italy, let alone between different countries and across continents.

'And why should there have been?' was the response of a spokesman for the Miami Police Department. 'To be frank, it would be like expecting us to share with Scotland Yard every time we had a complaint of someone pissing against a wall in public.'

That officer had a point. In the great scheme of things, someone snipping a few locks of hair as a prank or odd-ball trophy-hunting was small beer. There were serial killers to be caught, suicide bombers to be thwarted, drug-traffickers and people-smugglers to be nailed. Amid all the world's criminal mayhem and anarchy, the antics of a slightly weird but apparently harmless hair-cutter did not come close to inclusion on the international police-sharing network.

Like the Sicilian and American Mafia, the Camorra relied hugely on freelancers, known euphemistically as 'friends'. These 'friends' would be sub-contracted work according to needs and ability. Politicians, police officers and influential journalists – 'respected' commentators and opinion-shapers – were always required on the payroll. Of course, from the moment they accepted their first 'rotten' lira, they were fettered to the 'family' for life.

The previous year, Italy's Finance Minister took the extraordinary step of banning Philip Morris cigarettes. Since the Second World War, the Camorra had basked in a black market monopoly in Italy of Philip Morris tobacco to the tune of a £6 billion turnover per annum. Nearly half a million Italians earned a living selling those cigarettes. Several million smokers in Italy were only too delighted to avoid paying the government's 65 per cent tax on their favourite Marlboros. The number of smugglers flooding the market in the cigarettes via speedboats and trucks was estimated at 25,000.

Restivo always had boxes of Philip Morris cigarettes. Marlboros were a favourite smoke among the women, especially those in café society, so, to a certain extent, Restivo was able to ingratiate himself with some of the smart set. He once bragged in a bar that a college girl, convent-educated, had gone to bed with him just for a packet of Marlboros. If the story is true, he failed to see that it was an anecdote which didn't necessarily flatter him.

The Finance Minister even offered a government job for life to any Camorra tobacco-trader who would 'come clean' and 'grass' on the illegal traffickers. In Brussels, the European Commission declared the Italian Government in 'contravention of free trade' for its attempted ban on the Camorra's tobacco-smuggling racket.

The frustration of the Claps family was understandable, and tensions rose steadily as the days, and then weeks, dragged on without progress. Even the press started to wonder what the police were doing.

Mimmo Sammartino, friend of Gildo and editor in Potenza of the newspaper *La Gazetta del Mezzogiorno*, said, 'How is it possible that someone can disappear in broad daylight on a busy Sunday morning when people are going to church and no one saw what happened? It's beyond belief.' Mimmo added, 'Someone knows. There's a cover-up involved here, but that's nothing new. The usual suspects are in the frame, but what is missing, apart from Elisa, is the reason behind whatever's happened. Where has she gone? Who took her? What did she see or hear that was so important to protect? As a newspaper, we shall campaign to get to the bottom of this. As a friend, my heart goes out to the family.'

Crusading, fearless newspaper editors are to be admired, but in southern Italy and Sicily they tend to be regarded as foolhardy cannon-fodder. And their lives, and those of their loved ones, are significantly compromised.

Tearfully reminiscing about Elisa, Filomena said, 'She is the youngest of my family. I miss her sitting at the table. I miss her hugs. She was always so happy, always so loving. I often talk with her. We have conversations, in my head, as if she's in the room with me. In fact, she *is* here; I know it, which makes me sad because it means she can be here only as a spirit and will never walk through that door again.

'I'm lost without her. She's my first and last thought every day. I lay awake night after night thinking about her, wondering what she'd look like now. I never sleep. I've never slept since *that* Sunday. Lots of things happen in this town that are not good. You know about bad things, but you can't do anything about it, so you just get on with your own little world. Then suddenly it touches you and you can't ignore it any more.

'Elisa must have seen or heard something. She must have known something too much. Knowledge in these parts can be a dangerous thing. She was so young. She wouldn't recognise danger signs. Here, in Potenza, you have to think of life as a series of traffic lights. When they're on green, it's OK to keep going. When they're red, you look away, you stop, you turn around, you most definitely don't carry on. In between, you tread carefully, very cautiously.

'In Naples, there is shooting all the time. You hear gunfire day and night; in the hills, in the city, everywhere. I warned

Elisa about Naples. It's the Devil's city. Elisa wouldn't go there, not on her own, not by choice. I would never put one foot inside that city; Potenza's bad enough.

'My family tell me to keep my mouth shut for fear that something nasty will happen to me. I don't care. I kept my mouth shut all my life and look at my reward – I've lost my little one. *They* can do what they like to me now. I don't care about myself.

'The police aren't doing all that they could; not from day one. And we all know the reason why that is. We all know who's *really* in charge and who runs the town. Most of the priests are good men. They believe in God, like I do. But the Church is part of the system, part of the politics. It's how it's been since I have ever known it, and my parents, and their parents, and so on.

'I'm a simple person and I ask for simple answers. But there's nothing simple about how this region is run.

'Now, as soon as possible, I want to be able to close the book on Elisa and have somewhere to take flowers and to sit beside her, and smile, and hold her hand because, even if I can't see it, I know it'll be there. She needs a resting place. And then God can call me whenever he wants. I am ready to go. There is too much grieving here. I'm ready for a better place; I'm sure, in my heart of hearts, that Elisa has found it, though far, far too soon.

'The mysterious ways of God are too mysterious for me.'

Elisa's sister-in-law, Irena Nardiello, said, 'We have to accept there will be no happy ending. There's going to be a lot more anguish to go through.'

Then, suddenly, everything changed.

Elisa was spotted in Albania.

- 9 -

FAINT HOPE AND
WORST FEARS

The information seemed reliable. The police were not giving away too much, but a pithy statement intimated that they had every reason to believe that Elisa Claps was alive and in Albania, travelling with a male companion.

The reported sighting reputedly came from an Italian tourist in Albania who had seen photographs of the missing girl.

An Italian TV crew immediately flew to Albania. The TV journalists and their camera-team were only a few hours behind the officers of Italy's élite Anti-Mafia Unit, operating out of Salerno.

The location of the purported sighting, Albania, had touched a nerve among those determined to diminish the influence of the Mafia, hence the kneejerk reaction by the crack squad that had been formed to hunt down mobsters and to methodically and inexorably shrink their criminal activities.

Bear in mind that for months the general consensus throughout Italy was that the Mafia was heavily involved in Elisa's disappearance. If the mobsters had not themselves harmed her, they were covering for the person – or persons – who had. That had become a given. But why should they do that? The Mafia was not a charitable organisation. It had always been mercenary, introspective and ruthless. If it was protecting someone outside the Camorra, then it would be doing so only for its own benefit.

In view of all that was happening at that time in Italy with organised crime, the sighting in Albania made sense. For the Mafia-hunters, Albania fitted perfectly into the criminal food chain; it was a link that helped to complete the circle.

In her book, *Crime Without Frontiers* (Little Brown), Claire Sterling explored the elaborate route through which the Camorra's contraband tobacco was moved. Switzerland, Belgium and Holland were the countries where there were clandestine production facilities. From those countries, the outlawed goods were transported to Camorra storage depots in Hungary, Rumania, Bulgaria and Turkey. From the depots, the consignments were shifted to Yugoslavia and Albania, the final staging-posts before the illicit cargoes were shipped across the Adriatic to Italy. This was the 'Balkan Run' in reverse, the route for three-quarters of the black-market heroin into Western Europe. The 'Balkan Run' had also become infamous for the seizure of the largest convoy of bootleg weapons.

So the sighting of Elisa Claps in Albania, taken in context, was a natural trigger for the 'A' team to swing into action.

Elisa apparently had been seen setting off into the mountains. The TV crew interviewed anyone and everyone who had a story to tell. They recruited professional mountain-trackers; they hired a helicopter and an Albanian pilot; they showed hundreds of people photographs of Elisa. A few nodded, 'Yes, yes,' but the vast majority shook their heads. The trek turned into a comic tragedy, with as many different sightings and possible locations as there were people prepared to offer an opinion.

'We never really believed Elisa was in Albania,' said Gildo, speaking on behalf of the whole family. 'The TV people wanted to believe because it was in their interests to do so. They wanted to find her and bring her back and make world news. We wanted her back, too, of course, but we didn't allow our hopes to be falsely raised. We saw it for what it was.'

And what was that?

'To draw the spotlight away from Potenza,' asserted Gildo. In other words, someone was desperate for the world's attention to be drawn away from Potenza. In retrospect, it was probably far more specific and tighter focused than that. It is reasonable now to presuppose that it was the focus on the Most Holy Trinity Church that someone was conspiring to have deflected. Certainly it defied logic to imagine that the Camorra would deliberately draw attention to its contraband rat-run through Albania. The belief had to be that Elisa was being utilised as some kind of 'mule' by the Camorra and that must have taken some believing, even for a police force with virtually nothing else to go on.

It came as no surprise to the Claps family when the TV crew and the Italian police Mafia-hunters returned empty-handed from Albania. Back to square one … though not quite. Not back to the Most Holy Trinity Church, where the mystery began. The police were even more convinced now that the case would be resolved on the streets – either of Potenza or Naples.

The Claps family by this time was in no doubt that Elisa had been murdered.

The police, however, would accept no more than that she was a missing person and refused to raise the status level of the investigation, which meant that resources were kept to a minimum.

'There is not one shred of evidence to point to Elisa Claps having been harmed,' said a Potenza police spokesperson.

Too simplistic, criminologists in the UK and USA were saying. So many negatives in a case such as this must amount to a positive – no contact, no confirmed sighting, no cash withdrawals or plastic transactions, no apparent means of living, just a sudden full-stop. And to any experienced investigator, that had to imply a drastic and very unpleasant end. Unusually in this case, if anyone was in denial, it was the police and not the family of the missing teenager.

Complaints continued to come in about random cutting of hair, always while the victims were on buses or trains. A few of them were able to provide fairly detailed descriptions. With the help of two or three women, a police artist produced a drawing of the suspect. One officer noticed the likeness to Restivo.

The women were shown a photograph of Restivo and two of them were sure that he was the cutter. The two agreed to attend an ID parade, but Restivo travelled a lot and it was a few days before he returned to Potenza, by which time the women had changed their minds. They were no longer so sure; they had been 'hasty' with their initial identification, and they declined to try to identify the cutter in a line-up.

Then came the e-mail that was to break a mother's heart.

★ ★ ★

Filomena will never forget the day of the e-mail – it was addressed to her and the sender was claiming to be her missing daughter, Elisa.

The year was 1998. Elisa had been gone for half a decade. Years earlier, the Claps family had abandoned all hope of ever seeing Elisa alive again. And now this.

Without any overture or the slightest hint from the police, Elisa had surfaced, through the magic of modern technology. She had come home without making an appearance. Like a ghost, she had slipped into the house without passing through a door or window.

An e-mail is so different from a letter that drops on to the doormat. The presence of a letter is almost as good as having the sender momentarily with you as you read it. It is physical. You hold it. If the letter has been handwritten, you can connect with the flow of the thoughts and the heart. A letter, especially from a loved one, is so personal. But an e-mail simply announces its electronic, disembodied existence from the depths of a machine. Posted and delivered, almost simultaneously, with the press of a button.

Just visualise the scene that day. Heavy-hearted and sleep-deprived, as usual, Filomena slumped in front of the family computer – a new addition to her life that she was still coming to terms with – and logged in. Surfing the Internet had now become a daily habit of hers, like saying her prayers morning and night, but only in the hope of coming across a development in the case of her missing Elisa, something the police might possibly have overlooked, or forgotten to inform her about. But despite her willingness to embrace the latest technology, she had far more faith in the power of prayer than in the abilities of the police or the press.

Whenever there had been anything on the Internet reporting a new lead, it had never come to anything. 'Just reporters dreaming up something on a quiet day,' Gildo would say dismissively, and his mother would nod in agreement, eyes moist.

Filomena still cried every day. Her emotions were never completely in check. The heartache remained as insistent as it was the Sunday Elisa went to church and did not come home.

It had been a long time since anything of substance had been written about Elisa. She was old news; a cold case. Hers was also a statistic that embarrassed the police because there was still no explanation, only speculation.

On certain anniversaries, the media would rekindle interest, fleshing out the story with dubious new angles and the same old quotes from the police – 'This is not a closed file. We are still very active on the case. Any day now there could be a breakthrough. We're waiting for just one phone call, one tip-off …'

So Filomena was not anticipating any reference to Elisa on the Internet as she began her daily browse, and there was none, so she clicked distractedly on to her e-mail. There was a new one, identified in bold. Subject: 'Elisa'.

Her hand shaking, she manoeuvred the mouse and clicked again. She was so shaky that it took her several attempts to open the message, which began, 'Dear Mummy ...'

Dear Mummy! Instead of reading from the beginning, Filomena scrolled frantically to see which of her children had sent the missive. It was Elisa. Impossible!

Desperately trying to steady her hand, she steered the cursor back to the beginning of the message. Almost immediately, her hand shot to her mouth, as if to stifle a scream. Elisa, apparently, was safe and well. She was sorry she had caused so much grief to her family, but she just had to get away. Life within such a big family was claustrophobic, intolerable for her. She had been so unhappy, but she had not wanted to hurt anyone's feelings, so her solution had been to run away. Right away. As far away as possible.

Now she was living in Brazil, and everything was so different. She would never return. She pleaded with her mother to forgive and to forget her. She loved her family, but could not live with them. She had made a new life for herself on the opposite side of the world and she had made contact to put her mother's mind at rest. She regretted not having done this earlier, but warned, 'You won't hear from me again. This is hello and goodbye ... for ever.' She also stressed that she would not respond to any reply.

Hysterical and traumatised, her heart beating wildly, Filomena summoned her family around her for an emotional gathering. 'She's alive! She's alive!' Filomena gasped to each one of her large, extended family as they assembled to hear the news.

'Whatever did we do to deserve this?' she sobbed. 'Has she lost her mind? Perhaps she's had a nervous breakdown.'

One by one, they all read the e-mail.

Gildo, always a calming influence, was instantly sceptical. He told them all to 'look at this objectively'. He sneered at the 'this is hello and goodbye' line. 'It's so phoney,' he said. 'Does that sound like Elisa? It's something corny from a magazine. Would Elisa behave this way? Would she write this way to her mother?' All these questions were rhetorical. 'You could not have found a mother and daughter who were closer if you scoured the universe,' he said.

The problem for Filomena was that she wanted to believe; well, at least half of it. She prayed that Elisa was indeed alive, but did not wish to believe that her daughter had been driven away by herself and others in her close-knit family.

'What are you saying?' she said.

'I'm saying there's no proof that this e-mail is from our Elisa. How did she get to Brazil? How did she get into that country, without passport and papers, when every border authority had been primed to be on the look-out for her?'

One member of the family speculated that Elisa might have eloped with a Brazilian or had been kidnapped by the Camorra and sold to a tycoon in South America who had bribed immigration to issue her with legitimate domicile status. Bribery was rife in South America, it was argued. Protection from prosecution for any crime, even murder, could be bought. Riches could put any man or woman above the law.

Gildo was appalled when the Italian police seemed to be content to accept the e-mail at face value. 'It lets them off the hook,' he protested. 'They're able to say, "There you are, she *has* run off. She is a missing person, just as we suspected

Above left: Heather Barnett, who was brutally murdered by Danilo Restivo in her Bournemouth home in November 2002. She was discovered with a lock of hair in her hand. © *EPS/Rex Features*

Above right: Elisa Claps, the Italian teenager whose body was discovered in the roof of a church in the village of Potenza in March 2010 and provided a vital link to Heather's murder.

© *Bournemouth News/Rex Features*

Below: Elisa Claps' brother, Gildo, puts up posters in Bournemouth highlighting the links between the two murders.

© *Bournemouth News/Rex Features*

Above: Police move in on Danilo Restivo's home on Capstone Road in Bournemouth. Restivo lived on the same road as Heather.

© *Bournemouth News/Rex Features*

Below left: Heather Barnett's house – a set of keys to the house went missing shortly after Restivo came to see Heather about making curtains for him.

© *Peter Willows/Rex Features*

Below right: Danilo Restivo, the man with a sick hair fetish which ultimately led to murder.

© *Bournemouth News/Rex Features*

Above left: Police carried out surveillance on Restivo in the months leading to his arrest. This footage shows Restivo acting suspiciously at a local beauty spot. © *Bournemouth News/Rex Features*

Above right: Detective Superintendent Mark Cooper reads a police statement confirming that a man has been arrested in connection to Heather's murder. © *Phil Yeomans/Rex Features*

Below: Forensic teams at the home of Restivo.

© *Graham Wilding/Rex Features*

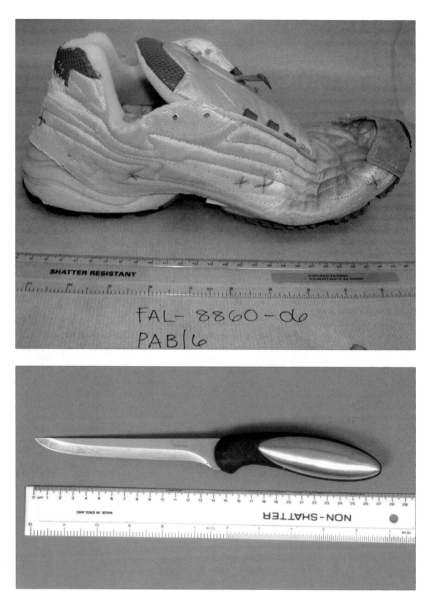

Vital evidence in the case against Restivo.
Above: Restivo's trainers were found soaking in bleach just days after
Heather was killed. © *Bournemouth News/Rex Features*

Below: A knife found in Restivo's satchel after he was apprehended
by police. © *Bournemouth News/Rex Features*

from the very beginning, and nothing more." It saves them a lot of work. They don't have to do anything. They say if we want to pursue the matter further, then we must take it up ourselves with the Brazilian authorities.'

Gildo was not prepared to be stonewalled. The Claps family was not wealthy, but Gildo had a friend who was a private investigator. A smart operator, too. The PI took on the case.

The Italian police in those days did not have a specialist, high-tech fraud unit. The PI consulted experts and quickly learned, what we all know today, that an electronic or computer trail is as trackable as any other – as visible as a vapour trail in the sky on a cloudless day.

It was not long before the PI had proved that the e-mail had been sent, not from Brazil, but from an Internet café in Potenza – just a few hundred yards from the Church of the Most Holy Trinity.

'But is it possible to establish who sent the e-mail?' Gildo asked his friend.

'Sure,' was the emphatic answer. A false identity could have been created, but ultimately there was no hiding place. However sophisticated the scams to conceal the true identity, a skilled cyber-tracker would be able to penetrate the mask.

'Trust me,' said the PI. And Gildo did. 'Remember this, whoever did send the e-mail wants you all to accept that Elisa is alive and well, living happily thousands of miles away,' the PI reminded Gildo.

'And we should stop looking for her?' said Gildo. 'We should just roll over?'

'Exactly,' said his friend.

All these quotes are as recalled and have been translated from the original Italian.

Within another week, they had conclusive proof that the e-mail had been sent from Potenza.

-10-

THE SPARK OF
AN OBSESSION

In June, 2006, Supt Phil James and a posse of senior
investigators from Dorset's crack Serious Crimes Unit
flew to Washington to pick the brains of specialist FBI
agents. The meetings took place in the FBI's Behavioral
Science Unit at the agency's headquarters in Virginia.

Founded in 1972, the unit was divided into three
divisions after 9/11: counter-terrorism and threat
assessment; crimes against adults; and crimes against
children. Recently, the FBI replaced 'criminal profiling' – as
so often portrayed in movies and in TV fiction – with
'criminal investigative analysis', and it was this area of
expertise in which James and his colleagues were interested.

From the outset of the investigation, it was accepted that
there had to be a history between perpetrator and victim,

however tenuous and flimsy, even if only in the murderer's distorted imagination. The killer had not randomly knocked on Heather's front door, and when she let him into her home there was nothing spontaneous or unrehearsed about what followed. He had planned with great care and forethought. He was no rampaging, psychotic madman — not the sort of caricature crazy who struts along a high street spraying everyone in sight with bullets from a machine-gun. More likely, according to the FBI, he was a semi-reclusive man, probably not yet in middle age, who was holding down a regular, but routine, job and apparently living a normal and rather uneventful life — a face in the crowd, and certainly not a head-turner.

The FBI advises on hundreds of cases of this nature every year. Mostly, the 'history' between slayer and victim was one-sided. They may have met only once; the victim may not have even remembered the encounter. But for the killer, it had become blown out of all proportion leading to irrational infatuation, and the belief that, for example, a simple, polite smile had been a 'come on'.

Psychiatrists in the community define stalking as repetitive, unwanted communication or approaches that induce fear in the victim, and are committed over a period of at least four weeks. For the investigating officers, however, undesired pursuit or contact on two different occasions is enough to constitute harassment.

One problem, however, as pointed out by the FBI, was that stalking is not always visible. In other words, the target is unaware that he or she is a quarry and, metaphorically, is in sharp focus in someone's telescopic sights.

Celebrities are notorious for attracting stalkers —

Madonna, The Beatles, Anna Ford, Steven Spielberg and Jodie Foster are but a few who have had their lives made a misery by deranged people who, on the surface and in their public persona, have appeared perfectly normal, which is probably the most alarming aspect of the stalking phenomenon. But the celebrity victims are only the tip of the iceberg. According to academic studies, one in every five GPs is stalked during their careers. The risk to psychiatrists is even bigger, which is perhaps not surprising. The overall picture in the UK and USA is very similar: 8 per cent of all women and 2 per cent of the male population will become the victim of a stalker.

The FBI revealed that 40 per cent of all stalkers have had a sexual or substantial emotional entanglement with the object of their obsession. However, 27 per cent were victims of total strangers, a statistic that certainly did not fit the Heather Barnett case – of that the Dorset Police were confident. Also, by now, they had eliminated all men who had had any form of established relationship with Heather. But neither, they were sure, had he been a total stranger.

The information from the FBI was disturbing. Stalkers frequently hired private investigators to shadow their victims in order to learn everything possible about their routines and habits, their friends, favourite pubs and restaurants. Telephones were tapped; dustbins were rifled. If used condoms were found, this was likely to knock stalkers badly off kilter. 'Bugs' were planted in houses, particularly in bedrooms, with access often gained by stealing door keys.

Stalking was often a sexual experience for the pursuer. Frequently, stalking amounted to a sex-substitute, producing an orgasm in many women stalkers and ejaculation in men.

They were all almost certainly control freaks, revelling in the power they believed they were wielding over the objects of their desires, explained the FBI. Mostly they were exacting revenge for some kind of perceived rejection, although it was usually imagined and had not actually occurred.

One subdivision of erotomania is known as 'de Clérambault's Syndrome' in which sufferers have a profound narcissistic tendency. Although some psychiatrists believe that such sufferers can be helped as psychiatric outpatients, the FBI remains dubious, because the condition is usually underpinned by schizophrenia, which could erupt out of control without warning.

Dr Thomas Stuttaford, a former Member of Parliament and a widely-respected, regular contributor to the *Times* on medical matters, has said, 'The erotomaniac's love is based on delusions. These delusions may be so fixed that they are not necessarily erased by a spell inside [prison]. There are well-recorded incidents in which a discharged prisoner immediately starts harassing the [same] victim again.'

De Clérambault gave his name to the syndrome characterised by erotomania, but he was not the first psychiatrist to profile it. Emil Kraepelin and Richard von Krafft-Ebing, both pioneering in their fields of psychiatry, had flagged up the essential features. Krafft-Ebing wrote in depth about the obsessive love that some people felt for someone distinguished – mirroring groupies who have gone several stages further than idolising and hero-worshipping. But more recent psychiatrists have disagreed with the Krafft-Ebing research, particularly over his contention that the one-sided love was always platonic or romantic. In other words, it was devoid of a sinister element.

Dr Stuttaford believed that Kraepelin was much more realistic, explaining, 'He suggested that erotomaniacs subconsciously or consciously perceived that the victim, usually someone in a position of importance and of higher social standing, was well-disposed towards them. This is where the delusion started; thereafter, every glance, every chance meeting between stalker and stalked was seen by the former to be evidence of hidden love. Every episode of their encounters in the obsessive person's mind provided evidence of a victim's infatuation for them. Even a victim's choice of clothes had a significance, and their conversations hidden meanings.'

As long ago as 1832, Dr Isaac Ray described how the erotomaniac stalker derived 'unbridled excitement' from a 'military-styled pursuit of the object of his desire'. It was automatically assumed that stalking was an exclusively male perversion, a notion whose shelf-life ended years ago.

As Dr Stuttaford further explained, 'Milder degrees of erotomania may be more distressing to the victim and the patient than those caused by an exaggeration of the normal emotions felt by lovers. Even otherwise rational people have been known to lurk around a former lover's house or office in the hope of seeing him or her.

'With obsessive love, stalkers are irrational, convinced that if circumstances had been different, the object of their obsession would be theirs. They are convinced that they have been thwarted by the actions of others. Their delusions are reinforced as words and actions are misinterpreted.

'Despite any lack of encouragement, they are certain that sooner or later their pursuit will be fulfilled. So great is their ability to rewrite history that they can convince themselves they were the pursued and not the pursuer. Unfortunately, they have so convinced themselves that they are able to persuade others.

'Men or women who may be merely colleagues or friends of the stalker's target may become targets, too. The stalker may believe that if only so-and-so were out of the way, the object of affection would be his or hers.

'A peculiarity of these attacks, whether only in the mind or actually fulfilled, is that the thought of them gives stalkers a sense of power. They enjoy inducing terror in wives, husbands, friends, partners or employees.

'Characteristically, the 20 per cent of stalkers who resort to violence give no prior warning.'

'In most cases,' said Dr Stuttaford, 'the object of the violence is the person stalked, but in a minority of cases it is a third party, an imagined rival, who is attacked.

'Violence is most commonly committed by those who feel themselves to be rejected partners, rather than those who are obviously psychotic.'

The British medical publication, Lancet, reported that in stalker-related assaults, a quarter resulted in murder. A further 15 per cent were failed murder attempts, while 30 per cent account for a combination of grievous bodily harm (GBH) and actual bodily harm (ABH). Therefore, most of the violence from stalkers was of a serious and life-threatening nature. Most stalkers are unquestionably seriously deranged and have to be feared as potentially capable of inflicting fatal injuries.

The FBI specialists warned that stalking was much more prevalent than most police forces either realised or acknowledged. They estimated that there were about 26 per cent of all stalkers with a psychotic illness such as schizophrenia at any given time and in any Western country. Bereavement was also, perhaps astonishingly, a trigger for stalking, especially if the death left a vacuum in someone's sex-life. Dr Stuttaford identified with this analysis, saying, 'Most stalkers are lonely and find relationships difficult. Alcohol use in both sexes, and premenstrual syndrome in women, may exacerbate the situation.'

Erotomaniacs, according to experts both sides of the Atlantic, frequently became obsessed with someone they considered of a higher professional or social standing. They lived the lie and sucked others into it.

Dr Stuttaford's final comment was very telling. 'The desire to exaggerate or to seek intimacy is very common and they not only convince themselves but others that whatever association there was between them was much greater than in reality.'

Was the trigger the day that Restivo called on Heather to negotiate over the making of curtains for Fiamma as a Christmas present? This visit was just a few days before Heather's murder. He told police that he had gone to Heather's flat at around 8.30am, before catching the bus to NACRO. He explained to her that he was in a hurry and did not have the time to discuss material and cost. It was arranged that she would phone him when she was not busy. However, the NACRO records revealed that Restivo had not gone straight to college by bus. The attendance register showed that he was absent without permission that morning. Other NACRO records indicated that he had claimed expenses for a car journey to NACRO.

It was after Restivo had left Heather's flat that she noticed her spare key to the front door was missing and immediately suspected him of having taken it. Later that same day, she slipped a letter, addressed to Fiamma, through her letter-box. Heather complained that she feared Restivo had stolen a key of hers. And in an e-mail to a friend, Keith Drew, she mentioned Restivo's visit and the fact that she had changed the lock on her front door because of the stolen key. Heather went to Restivo's house to take measurements for the curtains she was to make and later confronted him, in his home, about the key that had vanished mysteriously. He denied having been responsible for stealing it.

Fiamma had challenged Restivo about Heather's visit to the house while she was out, so he had to tell her about his plans for buying curtains for her as a Christmas gift. Apparently, Fiamma told him that she would not appreciate curtains as a present, so he abandoned the idea.

The Dorset detectives returned from the USA with new theories to be put to the test.

-11-

CUT AND RUN

The police in the Potenza region were becoming increasingly used to teenage girls absconding from home for the tantalising lure of Naples and all its gilt-edged temptations. Vanishing from the radar entirely was much rarer, however. Usually, it meant that a runaway had dropped out of society's lowest social class, and was now living rough on the streets, begging, or turning to prostitution. In those circumstances, the outcome was unpredictable.

Some of those young women, inevitably, would catch sexually-transmitted diseases, even AIDS, and succumb to its inevitable outcome without ever receiving, or indeed seeking, medical aid. The lucky ones would be arrested, identified and reunited with their parents, before receiving an appropriate sentence that would frequently involve long-term pastoral care and intensive counselling. At least in prison they would be fed hot meals, sleep in warm beds, and be weaned off drugs if addiction had become a problem, a common feature of most of these harrowing cases.

Violent death for runaways was always a risk. Some ended their lives dumped in rivers, in derelict buildings, on landfill sites or on waste ground, discarded like garbage. But sooner or later, they all surfaced, one way or another. Unless, of course, they had never run away in the first place. These are sobering thoughts when considering the undeniably lacklustre attitude of the police to Elisa Claps's disappearance.

Serious Italian police investigations were conducted in a similar fashion as in France, with magistrates involved from an early stage, frequently instrumental in choreographing investigations, something that had a direct influence on Restivo's actions and the final assessment by the police, who, in the first few years after Elisa's disappearance, remained entrenched in two opposing camps. The elder faction was more cynical and took the view that Elisa had taken off voluntarily, probably with a secret lover; there was nothing further to do except circulate her name, a photograph and a description. The file could be downgraded to a bottom drawer. But their younger colleagues were the hard-core disbelievers. They refused to accept the most obvious theory at face value

One of the magistrates in Potenza was as sceptical as the police disbelievers over the theory that Elisa had run away and somehow simply disappeared into the ether. Even the local media would not allow her 'ghost' to be forgotten and kept prodding the police, a thorn in their side, to do more.

The magistrate demanded that Restivo be arrested and brought before him. This was duly done and Restivo was ordered to repeat his account of what happened on the Sunday when he had had the clandestine rendezvous in church with Elisa.

As he listened incredulously, the magistrate, astute and forthright, asked searching questions, particularly relating to how Restivo had injured his hand. The magistrate said that he found serious inconsistencies in the story and harboured grave reservations about its veracity.

The way Restivo claimed to have damaged himself was at variance with the medical report. The magistrate openly accused Restivo of being a liar and gave him a chance to tender a plausible version; basically, to come clean and to own up.

But Restivo stood his ground and said he had no intention of recanting a word. He had told the truth and nothing but the truth. So there was a stand-off, but the magistrate in such a situation had the power to have the last word, which he did, resoundingly.

Restivo was charged with perjury and convicted in the Potenza Criminal Court of deliberately giving false information to the Prosecutor in relation to Elisa's disappearance. He had lied, in a sworn statement, about how he had injured his hand; he had also lied about his movements on that Sunday and about how Elisa had left the church before him. The sentence was custodial and, no doubt, the hope was that life behind bars would be so intimidating he might relent or be tempted to say something incriminating in the presence of other prisoners.

No such luck. Restivo, if indeed he really was the

perpetrator, was adept at maintaining his poker face. As one Italian officer said, 'If he is a killer, then he's the coldest-blooded bastard I've ever had the misfortune to encounter. He is truly scary, believe me. I've come across some Mafia assassins in my time, but none has been as Arctic as this one. He's the original Ice Man.'

The months passed and Restivo sat them out in gaol, finally being released after a little more than eight months. After his release from prison, Restivo saw no future for himself in Potenza. A new millennium would soon be dawning and he made the decision to leave Italy and head for Bournemouth where he had a friend with whom he could stay.

However, the cost of living in Bournemouth is one of the highest in the UK outside London. Property prices and rental charges are in Europe's super league. But if you were looking for a town or city in which to become 'lost' in the crowd, to remain anonymous even when English is not your native tongue, then Bournemouth has to be a perceptive choice. For many months of the year, the town is colonised by students, many of them mature, from all over the world. The Bournemouth/Poole conurbation has become a mecca for foreign students studying the English language, and private colleges have sprung up in huge numbers.

Bournemouth also held another attraction for Restivo – he had been building a relationship, via the Internet, with compatriot Fiamma Marsango.

Restivo moved seamlessly into his new lifestyle. He frequented the plethora of Italian restaurants and coffee bars; all the proprietors and most of the staff hailed from his homeland. Language was no barrier, even in the nightclubs, which had mushroomed all over the central sectors of the town, including Boscombe.

Danilo Restivo soon became a habitué of many of the clubs. There was certainly nothing reclusive about his lifestyle during this period, nor was there anything about his public persona to suggest that he was living a lie. The low profile that he had first adopted was quickly discarded. Swinging Bournemouth apparently had more to offer an Italian bachelor than even Naples, despite the fact that he was living with Fiamma as her domestic partner.

One girl, Carla Rosselli, who met Restivo at Elements nightclub, said, 'We had a lot in common, or so I thought, because I come from Florence and had visited Naples many times when on holiday with my parents. I was learning advanced English and doing Business Studies at one of the colleges. We talked in Italian. I told him it would be helpful for him to speak as much as possible in English, but he seemed very lazy. I pointed out that it wasn't a good idea to stick to a circle of friends of only Italians.

'I explained that everyone mixed in Bournemouth and there were no racial barriers among the young, but he should make the effort to learn the language so that he would integrate socially more easily.

'He never seemed short of money, even though he claimed to be a student, like the rest of us. When I asked what he was studying, he said something about dentistry, which seemed odd to me. I couldn't see how he was taking such a course if he didn't speak English. And why come to Bournemouth for that? It seemed to me that it would have been much better to have studied dentistry in Italy, but I wasn't interested in him enough to pursue it.

'But I guess you could describe him as something of a mystery man, which I think, on reflection, he might well have been trying to cultivate. He was very serious and intense; ill at ease in company and not the sort of guy you'd expect to find at a rave.

'When we were standing together, having a drink, he kept on about how lovely my hair was. "It's so smooth," he said in Italian. "So silky."'

Carla's hair was naturally raven-black, accentuating her classical Mediterranean features. She was 22 at the time and sharing a rented flat with two other girls – one Spanish and the other French. Her father was a lawyer and her mother a teacher. She and her flatmates always chatted in English. It was a house rule.

'The three of us were in England to become fluent in the language,' she said. 'Using it while socialising was an important way of improving usage. Getting to grips with colloquial English was the tricky bit and you couldn't learn it from textbooks.

'Although I was at first flattered by the comments of Danilo about my hair, I soon got bored because he had very little else to talk about. There was no real conversation. He had staring eyes and he began stroking my hair as if I was a dog or cat. I started thinking he was a bit creepy and I made an excuse to rejoin my friends. After that, he kept looking at me. However many times I moved, he always seemed to have repositioned himself so that I was in his sights. He'd asked for my address and mobile number, but I didn't give either of them to him, yet a few days later I would have sworn he was following me along the Wimborne Road.'

Wimborne Road was not far from where Heather Barnett and Restivo lived.

'He was alone, about 50 metres behind. I think he sort of smiled as I looked over my shoulder, but I didn't acknowledge him. I quickly turned away and carried on walking towards the town centre. I wasn't scared; nothing like that. Sort of more irritated. I was anxious not to give him any encouragement so that he wouldn't pester me for a date.

'I saw him once again, this time in a café bar and he was sitting at a table for two, opposite a girl, another student, I guess. They were talking in Italian. From her accent, I fathomed she came from the south. And would you believe, he was stroking her dark hair, like he was besotted or pampering a poodle. Just seeing him do that made me shudder. I was again with friends. He didn't even look up as we passed his table, so he didn't notice me.'

Carla extended her stay in Bournemouth after completing her college course, working in a large hotel overlooking the sea and then in a popular restaurant in the cosmopolitan Charminster Road area, within sight of the roads where Restivo and Heather Barnett were living. She has now returned to Italy to train as a lawyer. She had forgotten about the young Italian man with an obsession for women's hair until she saw his photograph on the front page of a regional British newspaper.

Another Italian woman, Sophia Pinot, also recalled how she, too, had a brush with Restivo in Bournemouth.

'It was between 3.30 – 4.00pm in the afternoon of a weekday. It could have been a Wednesday or a Thursday, I'm not sure, but it doesn't matter much. It was summer and warm. I was sitting next to a girlfriend on a bus, one of the yellow double-deckers, on the short journey from town to the middle of Charminster Road. We were babbling excitedly, the way we young Italians do, when I became aware of someone fondling, or caressing, my hair. I turned round and there was this guy sitting behind me, on his own, sort of grinning stupidly. I said to him, "Did you just mess with my hair?" He shrugged and made some remark about not understanding.

'I was angry. I have long hair and it hangs down my back. I could tell it wasn't an accidental touch. If he'd been just a boy, I'd have treated it as a juvenile prank, a joke, but this was a grown man and I knew he'd been deliberately playing with my hair. Technically, it was an assault, but nothing I could prove.

'I said, "Don't you dare touch me again." He shrugged, the same as before, then suddenly spoke in Italian. "I don't know what you're talking about," he said, which made me even more angry.

'I replied in Italian, "Liar!" The bus was full or we'd have changed seats, but we didn't have much further to go. The thing is, he got off at the same stop and started following.

'We went into a café and he stood outside, peering in, like a peeping Tom, for several minutes. The café was full of young people, mostly students from other countries. We felt safe in there, but still he just stayed there staring, like he was in a trance, transfixed. He was weird, but there were lots of weirdos about, especially after dark, though this was in the middle of a sunny afternoon.

'We must have stayed in the café for at least an hour and when we ventured out into the road, I had a good look around to make certain he wasn't anywhere in sight, such as in a shop doorway. He must have pushed off. Even so, we were cautious and kept stopping and looking around to satisfy ourselves that we weren't being followed. The main thing was to make sure he didn't find out where we were living.

'I never saw him again after that until his photo was published in a newspaper. I showed it to my friend. "I'm sure that's the freak who played around with my hair on the bus," I said. She held the newspaper close up to examine it carefully. She agreed. She said, "Yeah, I think you're right. It *is* him. Fancy that!" I said something like, "I told you all along he was a weirdo."

'We debated whether we should go to the police, but decided against it. To be honest, I wasn't keen on getting mixed up in anything like that. You never know what might happen to you. It attracts attention. Also, I wouldn't have been much help. I mean, he didn't cut off any of my hair; he didn't harass or molest me after we got off the bus. I thought I might sound a bit stupid and paranoid, especially as we couldn't prove anything. After all, neither of us actually saw him combing my hair with his fingers. And there's no law against watching people eat and drink in a café. We knew his behaviour was dodgy, but it could be made to sound nothing at all. As my friend said, the police must have had a lot stronger evidence than we could give and we couldn't really add anything new.'

Undoubtedly, the worst hair-cutting incident had been perpetrated in a cinema in Potenza. Restivo had been sitting directly behind a young woman and her fiancé. The woman kept feeling her hair being touched and tampered with, then cut. Whispering, she complained to her fiancé, who turned round to find Restivo with his genitals exposed and masturbating.

Naturally, the young man was furious and ordered Restivo to move away, preferably to leave the cinema immediately. There was no doubt about Restivo's identity because he was known to the families of the engaged couple, a fact that prevented a complaint being made to the manager of the cinema and the police. But the woman did go to the police after watching the Italian version of *Crimewatch*, in which an appeal was made for anyone who had suffered at the hands of a phantom hair-cutter. This appeal was included in a segment highlighting the case of missing Elisa Claps and calling for help from anyone who could throw light on her disappearance.

Restivo is known to have accessed online dating agencies, describing himself as a single, intelligent, professional Italian, who enjoyed the arts, literature, fine wine, dining out and convivial, but serious, conversation. He projected himself as cultured, preferring to avoid flippant or casual affairs. Anyone reading his self-promotion would have assumed that he was searching for a permanent relationship, so he was betraying Fiamma. He was certainly confident and sure of himself, something he did not mention. Some police officers were later to refer to him as 'cocky' and 'arrogant', but this could well have been because he proved such a hard nut to crack. Certainly, he was well versed in his legal rights within European law and came across as something of an amateur lawyer. Despite his Latin blood, there were never any overt histrionics from him when under pressure. All his actions and responses appeared calculatingly measured.

In Bournemouth, the police had substantiated beyond all

doubt that there had been a 'window of opportunity' for Restivo to have killed Heather Barnett. Restivo's alibi was peppered with holes. However, the timing would have had to have been spot on, carried out with the precision and determination of a military operation.

But could a man calmly arrive for a lesson, after having committed such butchery on a fellow human being? Could anyone appear to be so composed after cutting off his victim's breasts just a few minutes earlier, then changing clothes and cleaning himself up, then logging on to his computer and socialising as if it was just another ordinary, mundane day? Was it really humanly possible? Could it be sold to a jury, without it being dismissed as nothing more than far-fetched conjecture?

Answering these questions, one by one to themselves, the police knew, by the very horrific nature of the killing, that the perpetrator was capable of literally anything. He had to be merciless and inhuman, so the question of whether it was *humanly* possible was redundant.

Heather's house would have had to have been known to the man who had decided to take her life. However, the killer still had to be something of a chancer, because he could easily have been seen entering or leaving the house. There might even have been a customer inside already. One of the children could have been off school, sick. This last risk might have been eliminated by his watching the house earlier in the morning from a safe distance, observing Heather drive off with both children.

No matter how convinced the police were of the sequence of events that morning, they were equally confident that they could not prove them to the satisfaction of the Crown Prosecution Service, let alone a jury. They needed more. They needed a break, something that would move their case beyond reasonable doubt. Above all, they needed a stroke of luck.

Increasingly, they looked to Potenza. If Elisa Claps had been murdered, and there was a link to the killing of Heather Barnett, it might provide vital evidence.

-12-

STAB IN THE DARK

By 2004, Restivo had risen in stature within the Bournemouth Italian community. And it was now time for him to make a respectable woman of Fiamma if their relationship was to continue, for they had both been brought up in the Roman Catholic faith, the traditional religion of their birthplace. Fiamma had evidently made it clear that she would not continue to live with Restivo indefinitely without the relationship being solemnised in marriage. Hence their wedding in Bournemouth during the summer of that year, the culmination of a romance originally played out over the Internet, in true 'blind-dating' fashion, eventually leading to Restivo emigrating to the UK and building a life for himself and Fiamma on the South Coast.

With marriage came a certain respectability and status for Restivo as head of his own family unit. The marriage contract satisfied Fiamma's desire to live with Danilo Restivo as his wife, and also conferred on the couple the apparent gloss of decent, honest dependability that newlyweds seem to have in abundance. No longer living in sin, they were now legit – and they had a contract to prove it.

Neighbours of the couple described them as 'reclusive' and 'reserved', not displaying the customary Italian exuberance and flair for animated conversation. This hinted at quite a character reversal for Restivo. One woman said, 'They had their curtains drawn across the windows day and night, even in brilliant sunshine. They weren't what you'd call neighbourly. Whenever I heard them talking, it was always in Italian, which made it difficult for them to be a part of the neighbourhood. Of course, there always has been a big turnover of residents around us because so many of the properties are rented. A large percentage of the houses have been converted into flats for students. You can live here for ten years and never get to know your neighbours. A couple of times I said "hello" to them, but I never got an acknowledgment, not even a smile, so I didn't bother again. He always seemed preoccupied and they were an odd couple, but didn't cause any trouble. They certainly weren't a pain in the bum like some. I didn't see much of them and I don't think many other people did, either.'

A middle-aged man, who lived nearby, said that he had seen Restivo several times, but did not know his name until seeing it in a newspaper, underneath his photograph.

'He always seemed to be in a hurry,' he said. 'Quite a few times I saw him scurry out of his house in a flustered rush and he had a habit of always holding down his head, as if he didn't want you to see his face. He'd go to his car, stick a key in the lock of the driver's door, then glance up and down the road, kind of shiftily, as if to make sure no one was watching him. Of course, it could be that he was just extra safety-conscious and wanted to avoid opening the door into a passing car.

'Twice I saw him pull up in his car and both times he got out quickly, looked around him furtively as he locked up, and then hurried indoors, head down again. We're used to rum ones around here. They come and go, just like the tide ebbing and flowing, especially the students. But these were too old to be students. Mind you, we have students in this town who are already drawing their old-age pension. This fellow Restivo looked a bit of a wet to me, but I'm told by others that he was always very civil and was never any bother.

'The Italians around here have a reputation for being very generous, warm-hearted and family-loving people. Very respectful to women and always fussing over kids. After Mrs Barnett's murder, the police activity around here was intensive for years. The murder was almost the sole subject of conversation for months – and then around the anniversary of the crime every year. We were never allowed to forget and that was right and proper, I suppose, though unnerving. We all had a theory. There was bags of gossip. Much of it was hearsay stuff that got embellished into fact. The popular belief was that the police feared there was another Jack the Ripper on the loose. As far as I can tell, that was never something even hinted at by the police. It was the fear of the people around here, not a police warning.'

★ ★ ★

Some four months before Heather's murder, there was a crime that years later would be examined again.

In the early hours of 12 July 2002, a female student was jumped upon from behind and stabbed three times in the back. She was walking alone, after an evening with friends, along Malmesbury Park Road, yet another residential thoroughfare running parallel with Capstone Road and Chatsworth Road.

The student, Jong-Ok Shin, was a South Korean. To her friends, she was known affectionately as Oki. Aged 26, she was in the UK to study the English language at a college similar to the one Restivo was attending.

Oki had been to a nightclub with her friends. Bournemouth had become very popular with South Korean students. Many South Korean parents settled in the Bournemouth area purely to get their children into local grammar schools. An English education was considered an enviable status symbol in their country.

CCTV footage showed Oki leaving the nightclub happy and smiling. She had been drinking, but was not drunk. She was still with friends, but they must have soon split up, going their separate ways to their different flats. From various CCTV cameras dotted around the town, the police were able to tell that there was no one obviously following her.

Between midnight and 3.00am in summer, Bournemouth's centre is busier than most other large towns at midday, and considerably more intimidating. The clubbers are on the march – either in or out. Tourists help to swell the vibrant nightlife; hookers display themselves to passing motorists; and lurking in the shadows, gangs threaten tribal warfare.

Charminster, although on the fringe of the town centre, has its own style of international, vibrant nightlife; more restrained, more congenial, and less gaudy. Malmesbury Park Road, although an integral part of Charminster, would have been relatively quiet at that time of night. There was street lighting, shouts from the occasional drunk, and the sound of the odd squeal of brakes or over-ambitious acceleration. Night owls, like Oki, quietly picked their way home from the bright lights and the incessant thump of the clubs and bars.

Oki was almost home when she was ambushed from behind. Although she was alone, there were other people about, other students returning from a similar night out in town, who were soon to turn into the road where Oki was left gasping for breath, with her lifeblood draining away. More importantly, there was an apparent eyewitness.

The attacker did not have time to try to conceal the body. He took off and Oki was quickly discovered by passers-by. When the paramedics arrived, Oki was still alive – just. But before dying in Poole Hospital, she was able to tell detectives that her assailant had been wearing a mask.

This case, in its own way, was as strange as the Heather Barnett crime. The major difference between the two murders was that, in the case of the South Korean student, there was a quick arrest.

Omar Benguit, who lived in Winton, a northern suburb of the town, about half a mile from the crime scene, was 'fingered' by the alleged eyewitness, who happened to be a prostitute and drug-addict, well known to the police, frequently being arrested on street corners and cautioned.

Nevertheless, Benguit was charged with Oki's murder. Two juries failed to reach a verdict. Normally, that would have been sufficient for the case to be dropped. Quite extraordinarily, the prosecution decided to have a third attempt at securing a guilty verdict, subjecting Benguit to yet another trial. Nearly all the prosecution witnesses were drug-addicts, who were expected to recall events of almost three years earlier. However, at the third attempt, the prosecution achieved a guilty verdict and Benguit was sentenced to life in prison, with the judge stipulating that he should serve at least 20 years before being considered for parole.

This case was almost immediately seized upon by the Miscarriage of Justice Organisation (MOJO), branding it 'one of the most serious examples ever of injustice'.

The murder weapon was never discovered; there was no forensic evidence, DNA or otherwise, to associate the accused with the crime; and the police were unable to offer a motive at any of the three trials. The chief prosecution witness, who was a prostitute, changed her version of events at each of the trials and admitted to having lied in her first two statements. She even placed the stabbing on the wrong side of the road. Her reason for lying in her statements was that she said she had been afraid for her life, yet she had visited Benguit of her own volition after the murder and before his arrest. Her story included claims that she had been in a pub with Benguit when he talked in 'crude' language of fancying Korean women, which was contradicted by another witness.

Residents of Malmesbury Park Road had heard 'piercing screams'. But the Crown's drug-addict witness did not hear a sound from the dying woman, although 'much closer' to the stabbing than any of the people in nearby houses. She even took police to a river into which, she said, the murder weapon and bloody clothing had been thrown. Neither was ever recovered, despite dredging of the entire stretch of water and underwater searches by police frogmen.

Another of her accusations was that Benguit always carried a knife, something she did not think of until the third trial. She actually saw him sharpening one, she told the final jury. Naturally, she was asked for a description of the knife. The blade she described was totally different from the one that had cut into Oki, the medical evidence established.

Benguit lost his appeal. That was in 2005. Two years later, legal expert Barry Loveday, who was a reader of criminal justice studies at Portsmouth University, said, 'The case against Omar is simply not credible and is not backed by any forensic evidence. Shortly before Oki died, she stated that her attacker was wearing a mask, but the key witness made no mention of a mask. In my view, the wrong man was arrested and convicted, leaving the real killer still at large and a danger to the public. The chief prosecution witness gave a number of different versions and her accounts conflicted with those of independent witnesses.

In 2010, after Benguit had been languishing in gaol for eight years – two-and-a-half of them on remand between the murder and the third courtroom saga – his plight was taken up by international celebrity lawyer Giovanni di Stefano.

Hopeless cases were di Stefano's speciality and he scoured the world looking for them. Nicknamed 'The Devil's Advocate', he had always been unlike any other lawyer. He was a showman for whom the courtroom was a theatre. So often, though, his cue for an entrance on stage did not come until *after* the final curtain, as in the Benguit farce.

Di Stefano's love for lost causes had led him to some very high-profile cases – he defended such 'indefensibles' as warlord Slobadan Milosevic, Saddam Hussein, 'Chemical Ali' (Ali Hassan al-Majid), disgraced pop star Gary Glitter, Great Train Robber Ronald Biggs, Tariq Aziz, Charles Bronson ... and Moors mass murderer Ian Brady. And while Benguit was most certainly not in the same premier league of celebrity defendants, the miscarriage of justice element caught the maverick defence counsel's attention.

By April 2010, then, di Stefano was officially representing Benguit and announced on 26 April, via the *Austrian Times*, that he would be requesting a formal investigation by the CCRC, another UK public organisation with the remit of reviewing cases in which there may have been a miscarriage of justice.

'The Devil's Advocate' was in no doubt that the murders of Oki and Heather Barnett were inextricably connected. He reasoned that they were linked by the absence of any forensic clues; they were linked by location; and most compelling of all, they were linked, he claimed, by a lock of hair clasped in Oki's hand, something that had never been mentioned in the trials by the police or the prosecution, nor in any news coverage.

The showman subsequently stepped into the limelight yet again.

-13-

UNDER THE MICROSCOPE

In June 2004, the year of Restivo's marriage, the enigmatic Italian from sleepy Potenza was arrested at his home in Bournemouth by the senior officers investigating Heather Barnett's murder.

In a stereotypical dawn raid, a fleet of police cars swooped on a slumbering Chatsworth Road. Wearing just a white shirt and slacks, Danilo Restivo was bundled into the rear of the lead car and driven to Poole Police Station. He was aged 29 then and appeared totally unfazed and sanguine as he was taken into custody. He told detectives that he had nothing to hide and was happy to be interviewed. He was not a man with a burden on his conscience, he stressed. He would do all he could to assist them because, by doing so, he would clear his name and prove, once and for all, that he was a law-abiding citizen, proud to be living and working in the UK.

For three days, he was interrogated relentlessly but fairly under caution and in the presence of an interpreter. The questioning also included details of the disappearance of Elisa Claps. Old issues were revisited remorselessly. Yes, he did go to church for a secret meeting with Elisa Claps. No, he had not been with Elisa for long on the Sunday she vanished. No, he had not touched or seduced her that day, let alone harmed her. Yes, there was a special relationship between them, but nothing sordid or sexual. She was an unhappy, solitary girl and he had befriended her – was that unlawful? Were Good Samaritans deemed to be criminals these days? He had become someone she could trust, someone who wanted to keep her out of trouble and somehow to improve the quality of her life. Of course he was distressed by her disappearance, but how could he be expected to pinpoint her whereabouts if the police could not? No, he had not knowingly kept the company of underworld figures in Italy. He was hoping for a career as a dental technician within the health service, and was not someone who destroyed other people's lives.

As for Heather Barnett, he hardly knew her. He had been given Heather's name and address when he wanted a job done. He had been in her home only to have work done for him; that was all. Meetings with her had been trivial, not memorable. Why should they be? Who can remember everything about when they go to the shops? Of course he had not harmed her. What reason had he for doing that? She was a friendly, mumsy lady; nothing more to him. He had never been attracted to her sexually. He could never contemplate doing dreadful things to her.

'Such as what?' he was asked.

Such as what he had read in the newspapers, he answered.

What had he read? The police were hoping he would refer to something that they had not so far released into the public domain. But he astutely avoided all the investigative traps, sticking rigidly to his story. He had not been near Heather's house on the morning of her murder.

If he had been to Heather's home and committed such abhorrent acts, he could not have avoided leaving forensic identification. Where was that evidence? They were as bad as the Potenza police – all hot air, full of accusations, but offering nothing with which to back them up. He had been completely frank with everyone. For example, he had not tried to hide the fact that he and Elisa had been alone for a few minutes in church but, when they parted amicably, she had been alive and well. Was there any evidence to the contrary? No. Could anyone say for sure that she was not still alive and well? No. He was being persecuted because he was a soft target. He was being hounded in Britain and Italy because the police in both countries were bereft of ideas. They had no other suspects, so they kept pestering him to justify their existence and to keep the cases in the public eye. He was being exploited for propaganda purposes, but they were wasting their time. In 20 years, they would be no nearer to closing the cases if they did not learn to think laterally and to widen their net. They were stuck on a treadmill. They were welcome to search his house and to examine his clothes, as long as they refrained from planting anything incriminating. He knew all about corruption in certain police forces.

He had no history of violence; no criminal record of a

sexual nature. It was inconceivable that someone with such a clean sheet could go, in one leap, to being a sadistic monster. It flew in the face of all personality-profiling logic.

He was taunting them. They called his bluff and searched his home and garden. They questioned him further. Time was running out. They would have to charge him or let him go.

Supt James and his colleagues conferred. In truth, they had nothing substantial, nothing to secure the go-ahead from the Crown Prosecution Service. Even the circumstantial evidence was flimsy. Everything else could be dismissed as a series of coincidences. All right, there was no such thing as a 'coincidence' as far as the police were concerned, but that carried no weight in court.

One of the matters he was specifically quizzed about was the trainers that he had scrubbed with bleach. His explanation was that he had decided to wash the trainers 'in disinfectant' because they 'smelt horrible' due to the plastic. And when asked to explain his alleged suspicious behaviour in May at Throop Mill, which was videoed by undercover officers, he made no comment.

So, after three days in custody, Restivo walked out a free man. The police were hoping that the pressure was unnerving him and, sooner or later, he would cave in. Instead, he seemed more steeled. They had locked him up in Italy, accusing him of being a liar and perjurer. And in Bournemouth, he had been equally stoic and mentally resilient, soaking up all the accusations without weakening in the slightest. He became even more emboldened and this was probably a true reflection of his self-esteem. He had grown in stature, rather than being diminished. If the police were counting on his doing something silly, like panicking and decamping, they had misjudged him completely.

As one detective said, 'I reckon he must have had his nerves extracted when he lost his milk-teeth. On a scale of nought to ten, I never saw fear in his eyes rise above zero.'

After being released from custody, he picked up the thread and rhythm of his life as if he had simply been away on a relaxing mini-break. And while this may not have been the investigators' intention at the time, their prime suspect's new-found sense of superiority and complacency could well have proved to be his undoing.

★ ★ ★

As the authorities became gradually more and more concerned over the similarities between the cases of Heather Barnett and Elisa Claps, so a bond developed between the two families.

Gildo, Elisa's brother, travelled to Bournemouth. 'Somehow I felt that if I knew as much as possible about what happened to Heather in England, I might understand more of what had become of Elisa,' he said. 'It's hard to explain, I know, and doesn't seem very logical, but in Bournemouth I experienced a closeness with Elisa.

'I don't know what I expected to find to find in Bournemouth. Perhaps a feeling of getting nearer to the truth. Perhaps a feeling that Bournemouth was the place where the truth now rested. Our whole family had come to terms with the fact that there would be no peace of mind for us until we had the truth. The search for the truth had become our holy grail. Our quest.

'My mother's biggest fear was that she would die before Elisa had been found. She prayed on her Rosary until her fingers were raw. We have a simple faith. We believe that goodness and righteousness will prevail and eventually be rewarded. I have to admit that a part of me thought that I might find Elisa in Bournemouth. Of course, it was a forlorn hope and not based on any rational reasoning. There was nothing to suggest that Elisa had run away to Bournemouth.

'Long ago, we, the whole family, had resigned ourselves to the fact that Elisa was dead. Having her body for a proper Christian burial was the most we could hope for. And yet … yes, in a deep repository of our souls there was a little candle of hope flickering.

'I had a need to meet Heather's family. There's therapy in the sharing of suffering and grief. They understood what we were going through. We appreciated their pain, their loss.

'I knew, of course, about a suspect in Bournemouth. I knew that if he had killed Heather, he almost certainly had taken Elisa from us. I knew also where he lived. There had been much publicity. I had an urge to go to his house, bang on his door … But the police warned me to stay away. They said I would do more harm than good and that it would hinder any progress, rather than speed it up. They were right, of course, and I didn't do anything stupid. We are passive people, not aggressive.

'Before I set out, my mother made me promise not to let down the family. I gave my word. In Italian families, the mother rules; she's the boss. Mamma says do something, you do it. Mamma says don't do something, you don't do it.

'The one thing I could do in Bournemouth that was constructive was help to generate publicity. Get the public thinking about what they'd seen and heard. The hair-clipping fetish seemed to be the biggest clue the police had. It could have happened to many women who hadn't yet come forward. Maybe they were too shy or embarrassed. But one of them could possibly know exactly who did it and would identify him for the police. It could be the woman whose hair had ended up in Heather's hand in death.'

By now there were so many reports of women having had their hair shorn by a stranger in public places, usually on a bus or train, on numerous continents, that it was not feasible for one perpetrator to have been responsible. There had to be copycats. The police were having to consider the possibility of an international network, such as seen among paedophiles, rings of hair-snipping 'bandits' who might exchange locks of women's hair. Could it be that there was more than one killer indulging this hair-snipping fetish? Bizarre as it seemed, it had to be seriously tested.

After all, the circumstances of the two cases were already bizarre beyond belief. But if there was such networking, as with paedophiles, they would have to be communicating with each other via the Internet. And here the FBI led the world in cyber-surveillance. They had an entire unit dedicated to electronic 'tailing'– assessing, identifying and then logging suspect messages and images that were despatched, with a touch of a button, from one country to another.

The 'copycat' possibility spawned another fear – any copying of the hair-snipping could lead to copying of the murder. The police feared the worst, but hoped that they would find a breakthrough before things became much, much worse.

Daily, new reports were filed of other hair-clipping incidents on public transport, but Restivo could not have been the culprit — he was being closely watched. The FBI went to work with their techniques for interception, but were unable to uncover any organised network, and certainly nothing appeared to suggest any traffic on Restivo's personal computer to incriminate him.

While in Bournemouth, Gildo talked a lot about his mother and how she was finding the strength to 'journey through each heartbreaking day'. He explained, 'She desperately wants a resting place for Elisa, somewhere to take flowers and to sit and talk to my sister. Elisa may be dead, but not in our hearts and memories.'

In Potenza, Gildo had displayed throughout the town more than 100 posters bearing photographs of his sister and Heather Barnett, with the emotional caption underneath, 'We will remember them'.

Talking of the moment she first heard of the Heather Barnett case, Gildo's mother said, 'My immediate thought was for her children. I understand how they must feel. I wish I could meet them because they have lost a loved one, too. I want to make them believe that their mother is still with them. I still have Elisa, but not physically, not so that I can hug her, something I miss so terribly. Heather's children must feel the same about their mother. They must miss their daily hug. The emotional cord between a mother and her children is never broken.'

★ ★ ★

The cooperation between the police in Dorset and Potenza

was spontaneous. Once begun, the two-way transfer of information resembled a shuttle service.

The killer had been fiendishly clever in Bournemouth on 12 November 2002, but there was good reason to believe that he had not been so smart back in 1993 in Potenza. For a start, DNA profiling and matching had come a long way since then. A cautious, premeditated killer, such as a professional hit man, would have been careful not to leave fingerprints, footprints or samples of his blood, but he would have seen no danger in saliva, fibres or particles left from clothing. And, of course, he would have been right at that time. But by 2002, forensic science had progressed by leaps and bounds, something Heather Barnett's murderer obviously knew all about, hence his meticulous removal of all DNA material at the crime scene in Capstone Road, Bournemouth. However, there was nothing the killer could do retrospectively about any clues lying dormant in the Most Holy Trinity Church, Potenza. He could only hope that the body of Elisa Claps would remain undetected, as it had done already for so many years.

The British DNA database was initiated in 1995. By the year 2000, the database held 750,000 DNA profiles of people with specific criminal convictions. But the year 2000 was an important milestone, seeing the launch of an expansion programme that would include the entire British criminal population on the database.

Until 2001, any suspects who were not prosecuted or who stood trial and were acquitted would have their profiles wiped and all DNA samples destroyed. Just prior to 2001, a rapist and a murderer won their cases at the Court of Appeal because their profiles had been retained on the database from previous crimes. The reversal of the verdicts was based on a technicality, a loophole that had to be closed. The retained DNA samples had clearly linked them to the serious crimes with which they had been charged and convicted. However, from 2001 it became legal for all DNA samples to be stored indefinitely and, to date, there are almost 4 million names on the database and profiles from 300,000 crime scenes.

A further change in the law came two years later, with the Criminal Justice Act decreeing that everyone arrested for a 'recordable offence' must allow a DNA sample to be taken and kept for posterity. If a defendant refused, a sample could be obtained by force, usually by cutting off a few strands of hair. Soon Britain was the world leader in DNA technology relating to crime detection.

Most people – probably wrongly – assumed that the UK's national DNA database was housed in Scotland Yard; if not, then certainly somewhere within the metropolis. In fact, the headquarters were in the unlikely setting of an unprepossessing industrial estate in the West Midlands. The building was nondescript; red-bricked with nothing on the outside to give an inkling of the cutting-edge practices within its walls. The database expanded at the rate of 2,000 profiles every day and comprises more than five per cent of the UK population at the time of writing.

Most people by now know that DNA – deoxyribonucleic acid – is a chemical that is present in every human body cell, and stores all the information about our genetic make-up and history, everything that determines our physical appearance, including the colour of our eyes, hair and skin.

Like fingerprints, no two DNA patterns are exactly the same, except in the case of identical twins.

A DNA sample becomes a profile by an automated scientific process, producing a unique string of numbers, which are then fed into the database. So sophisticated has the science become that a single bead of sweat would be enough for a complete DNA profile. The relevance of this is that the tiniest amount of dried sweat – perhaps from a perspiring, murderous hand, left unwittingly by the killer of Elisa Claps, all those years ago in the Most Holy Trinity Church, if indeed that was her fate – could be sufficient to identify and then convict an abductor or killer.

Of course, most of those ground-breaking scientific techniques were still a world apart from remote police departments such as those in Potenza. But this was to become the major area of focus for the Dorset Police and their Italian counterparts. If Elisa Claps's body had been found quickly in 1993, vital evidence – microscopic, perhaps, and invisible to the naked eye – might well have been destroyed or unknowingly disposed of. The delay, although distressing to Elisa's mother and the rest of her family, was, in fact, a disguised blessing for the investigators, who now had so much advanced technology at their fingertips, thanks to the British investigation team.

Naturally, there was still some professional and territorial jockeying for position. The Potenza authorities were eager to maintain their grip on the Claps case, while not wishing to spurn the foreign assistance that could prove invaluable in bringing closure to one of Italy's most tantalising missing person's cases. Equally, the main motive for the Dorset Police helping to solve the Potenza crime was to establish the connection with Heather Barnett's death, resulting in an arrest and conviction in the UK. In a way, a race was developing between the British and Italian investigation teams to see who got the same man into court first.

But while some might argue that healthy completion was probably a hugely beneficial motivating factor, both police forces ultimately wanted the same thing – and they were to make use of evidence harvested many years earlier to get what they wanted.

Once the technology had been developed to identify almost 'perfect' DNA matches, police forces in the UK quickly saw the potential in the advancement of DNA profiling in bringing successful closure to many 'cold cases'. Some forces were a lot quicker than others in utilising this new crime-solving tool. Dorset had been at the cutting edge of the latest technology right from the early days of DNA profiling, something that proved to be a lucky break for the Italian police and Elisa Claps's family. From the moment the police started to investigate whether or not there was a link between the murder of Heather Barnett and Elisa Claps, the Dorset Police made all their expertise and technological resources available to the Potenza investigators. It was an offer that was too good to be refused.

Despite the lapse of time, there had not been one day when the Heather Barnett investigation was consigned to the back burner. Supt James regularly went public to reiterate that the investigation remained current and ongoing. Progress was being made, but by small increments. This case had matured into a game of patience, a perfect example of a modern police team combining the best practice of old-fashioned door-to-door enquiries and pounding the beat with ground-breaking, high-tech laboratory techniques that just a few years previously would have belonged to the world of science-fiction.

In contrast with the Heather Barnett file, Elisa Claps's vanishing act was very much a 'cold case' in terms of proactive initiatives. Until the involvement of Dorset's detectives, the Potenza police were still refusing to upgrade Elisa's disappearance from that of a purely missing person – a probable runaway – to that of a murder hunt. They were stuck in a time-warp – no corpse, no case.

The 'Dorset deal' was unique – their technology could unravel a foreign 'cold case' that, in return, could lead to solving a more recent British murder: symbiosis at its best and most practical. British journalist David James Smith gave a remarkable insight into DNA forensic procedures in an article he researched and compiled for the *Daily Telegraph*. 'The Forensic Science Service (FSS) routinely kept all the crime-scene stains submitted for examination, an untold number of files and microscopic slides, warehoused at room temperature and largely not degraded by time,' he wrote.

DNA samples, it seemed, could even outlive the memory of the crime. Dorset Police received funding from the influential Police Standards Unit (PSU), initiated by the Home Office, which published a manual of good practice for 'cold case' reviews. A single search on the DNA database could cost a force £5,000. Smith reported that half of the UK's 43 police forces had established 'cold case' units.

On a technical note, he further wrote, 'The process of storing crime-scene stains was unchanged over the years; they were transferred on to glass microscope slides and fixed and protected with a cover. In that way, now, as in the past, undetected cases were preserved in readiness for future scientific advances.'

The Potenza police were 'sold' on Britain's forensic trailblazing by the outcome of one case in particular that underscored the ability of British detective scientists to bring to justice the perpetrators of old crimes that had become dimmed by the passage of time. In the 1990s, a particularly violent assailant had been dubbed the 'Dearne Valley Shoe Rapist'. He had attacked and raped at least six women near Rotherham in South Yorkshire and had stolen their shoes – that was his trademark. The shoe fetish, of course, was the hook that inevitably made headline news.

South Yorkshire's police had even deployed one of its women officers, Sue Hickman, as a decoy. She would walk the streets at night wearing colourful shoes with stiletto heels, hoping to entice the rapist into choosing her as his next victim. She was wired and back-up was never far away. It was the kind of honeytrap that might work successfully in Hollywood movies. The 'Dearne Valley Shoe Rapist', though, spoiled the plot by not following the police script. Hickman walked and walked until her feet were so sore that she was blistered and limping, but the bait did not produce a catch.

The last rape in the series was in 1986. Hickman was promoted to Detective Sergeant and the 'shoe file' gathered dust, although she and other officers refused to allow it to disappear completely from their radar.

Then, in 2001, they submitted their samples from the case to the Forensic Science Service (FSS) at Wetherby. Three matching profiles came up from the assaults, proving that all the rapes had been committed by one man. Unfortunately, there was no match on the database, hence no suspect. But a year later, the BBC's *Crimewatch* programme featured the 'shoe rapist' case. An e-fit was shown, which bore a striking resemblance to the actual perpetrator, James Lloyd, a pillar of respectable society and a high-ranking Freemason. But no one identified Lloyd. The TV programme refreshed people's memories, but did nothing to bring about an arrest.

Another year elapsed and then Hickman and her colleagues heard about a new forensic search tool: 'Familial DNA'. The basis of the technique was that the DNA of relatives was more similar than that of strangers; not exactly rocket science. But applied to crime detection, it had special significance. For example, the 'shoe rapist' might himself not have been on the DNA database, but if a relative was, it could lead the police to the offender they were looking for.

A further three years went by before Hickman had a 'shortlist' of 43 names of possible sibling matches. It was still a long shot. There was no guarantee that any of them was a relative of the rapist. But as luck would have it, James Lloyd's sister was on the database, although, initially, there was no indication that she had a brother. But after revealing the existence of James Lloyd he was in custody within hours, after he had tried to hang himself, knowing that the net was closing in.

Later, in a statement to the police, he said, 'I was a bastard 20 years ago.' He had a collection of 124 women's shoes – many of them 'trophies' from his victims – hidden at his place of work. All but one of his victims was in court in Sheffield to hear him sentenced to life in prison, with a minimum 15-year tariff.

The Dorset detectives were able to convince the Potenza

police that a body in their town could be instrumental in solving a murder in Bournemouth and vice versa. Britain's history in leading the world in DNA profiling provided a learning curve for the Italians, and their support was quickly won over.

With this new-found international collaboration, both investigative teams believed that their respective cases now had a very good chance of being solved – and soon.

-14-

ENDGAME

By midway through 2006, the Dorset team were becoming both impatient and frustrated. There was a general feeling that they were so close to a result and yet were stuck in an impasse. The mood remained upbeat, though; there was no lethargy or defeatism. And not for one moment in any day was there doubt about the final outcome.

Nevertheless, the war of attrition was taking its toll. With no real breakthrough forthcoming, the investigators decided that the time was right to reinvigorate the investigation and try an entirely new approach, one that could possibly involve everyone in the country. So, in the September of that year, the police negotiated for the case to be aired on the BBC's hugely popular and successful *Crimewatch* programme, which had an amazing record for jolting people's memories and initiating the wrapping up of cases swiftly and dramatically.

The Dorset team were brimful of optimism. Police chiefs nationwide talked up the chances of a TV-inspired breakthrough. The success rate of *Crimewatch* gave detectives every reason to be optimistic.

Initially, the result was disappointing, with the feedback of poor quality. Little was learned that was not already known. Quite a few amateur sleuths phoned to talk through their theories and, as always, a number of cranks had their rant but, overall, the follow-up failed to generate the conclusive, eye-witness evidence the detectives were hoping for.

'We were hoping for something more,' said Supt James, a shade deflated. Another officer said, 'It would be wrong to call it a setback. We haven't gone backwards; we've simply been left treading water. You never know, there could be a delayed reaction. Someone could be mulling over whether or not to pick up their phone to give us a call. People don't always react reflexly [sic]. They often prefer to get it sorted in their heads before making a commitment; we understand that. We can wait, we're used to it. Time's on our side. This file will only be closed when there's a conviction.'

While waiting for that one call out of the blue, Supt James flew to Italy in the November to appear in the Italian version of *Crimewatch*, which was more fruitful. Lots of women responded, recounting disturbing experiences at the hands of a hair-cutting stranger. Several descriptions of the cutter tallied. The incident in the cinema came to light then, which resulted in Restivo being positively identified. And there was a distinct resemblance to Restivo in all descriptions of the phantom cutter, so James decided to turn up the pressure.

Consequently, another dawn raid followed. Restivo was arrested in Bournemouth for the second time. Once again he maintained his composure. He had heard about the Italian *Crimewatch* programme and he hoped it would be helpful to the police. And like Elisa's family, he was anxious to learn what had become of her. He had watched with detached interest the relevant British *Crimewatch* edition and he was as disappointed as anyone that it had not led to an arrest in Dorset. The fact that he was under arrest at that very moment conveniently escaped him.

The information from women who responded to the Italian show failed to touch a nerve with Restivo. He parried question after question. His rebuttal was the same as before — he was innocent and it was up to the police to prove otherwise. Implacable as ever, his underlying message throughout was a repetitive 'charge me or release me'. This time, Supt James did not bother to keep him in the cells for even one night.

Although Restivo was allowed home that evening, he was now on police bail. The screw was being turned. James was now liaising daily with Italian detectives.

And there, just as they were on the brink of despondency, the breakthrough came. Claire George, an assistant in a Bournemouth chemist shop, had seen *Crimewatch* and was adamant about the identity of a man in a black beanie-type hat crossing Charminster Road, heading towards Capstone Road, at 9.24am on the morning of Heather's murder. It was Restivo, a customer she had served regularly. If she was right, and she was prepared to swear on oath to the fact that she was not mistaken, then Restivo's alibi was blown apart. On its own, it would not prove that Restivo had committed murder, but it would establish him as a liar over crucial details; not only that, stripped of the protection of his alibi, it would give him the opportunity. And why lie about his movements on that all-important morning if he did not have a dark secret to hide?

The investigators were ecstatic, but the champagne remained on ice. Their quarry was still at large, now firmly in their sights, but tantalisingly just out of range. For the detectives, there was still a long haul ahead of them and it was essential that they retained the psychological edge. Time was on their side now. If any nerves were going to crack, it would be those of the killer.

In the new year of 2007, the year that Supt James retired, the Dorset team flew to Rome. Now, with Det Supt Mark Cooper in charge, they were furnished with copies of statements from women who had had their hair snipped in public. And in Italy at the time, there was a groundswell of unrest from the general public. The media was stepping up its criticism of the National Police Force. There was an organised campaign for action, with a lack of confidence in the police igniting both interest and concern among the ranks of politicians and women's movements. Giuseppe Persano, a police spokesman in Potenza, said that the working relationship between his force and the Dorset contingent could not have been more amicable.

The missing person theme, for so long the explanation of the Italian police, was beginning to look like a miscalculation. National and regional newspapers in Italy were now starting to question the competence of their nation's law enforcement agencies. So much so, in fact, that Franco Roberti, the chief prosecutor in Salerno, and his deputy, Rosa Volpe, the lead lawyer on the case, assured the Italian public that the investigation was constantly being reviewed.

Meanwhile, in Britain, the tempo of the police's efforts was being raised by the week. In the last month of 2007, the *Crimewatch* production team put together a second appeal that was aired with a full reconstruction of Heather Barnett's murder. It was undoubtedly an ordeal for the children, but the killer must have been tempted to believe that the investigation was foundering, yet again.

The New Year dawned uneventfully on the Heather Barnett case. And as the investigation entered its sixth year, the detectives were only too aware of the odds stacked against them. The likelihood of a successful outcome started diminishing significantly only 48 hours after the crime had been committed. After six years, technically this was indisputably a 'cold case'; worse than that, in fact, it was a case frozen in time. Soon there would even be a generation gap, something that could already be said of the Elisa Claps's mystery. There were teenagers in Potenza who had not been born when Elisa suddenly disappeared.

Still the Dorset team resisted any negative thoughts; the investigation was as active as if the crime had occurred only the day before. With Claire George's testimony in the bag, there had been a significant step forward, and at least things were moving in the right direction.

And then there was yet another sudden, unexpected twist in October 2009. Restivo went to the police to claim that his life was in danger. A package, addressed to him, had arrived in the post. Inside were two highly-polished, bronze bullet cartridges. And a message – a death threat. This was one calling card that he, as an Italian from the South, knew all about.

This bore the hallmark of the Mafia.

Restivo demanded protection. He was a victim, he said. Someone was intent on killing him. Here was the proof that he was an innocent man. If any harm came to him, his wife would have a valid reason for suing the police for enormous damages for dereliction of duty, for not having acted over the clearest possible indication that he was an intended target.

Restivo also contacted the Italian police, saying that they were obliged to investigate, just as much as the British authorities. They should trace the origin of the cartridges before the potential assassin had a chance to act. Naturally, the police agreed to look into the matter ... though perhaps not for the reason Restivo might have wanted.

This development intrigued the Dorset detectives. As for giving Restivo protection, he was already being closely 'chaperoned', albeit covertly and not specifically for his safety.

Almost the first question the police had for Restivo was the obvious one: 'Who could possibly want to kill you?'

Restivo's answer was that it was a spin-off reaction from all the negative publicity he had received, especially in his homeland, where violent retribution was a historic tradition.

But how would they know his address in the UK?

Via the Internet, he speculated. The road in which he lived had appeared in reports in the Bournemouth *Daily Echo* newspaper and it had been available online, apart from the house number. However, a search on the Bournemouth

Council's website, scrolling the electoral roll, would have revealed the full address in a matter of minutes.

Restivo did not hesitate to emphasise that members of Elisa's family knew exactly where he was living. So was he accusing the Claps family collectively, or singularly, of being instigators of a death plot against him? He had no idea, he said, but it was the duty of the police to investigate every possibility. Certainly the family had a motive, he argued. They believed he had done something terrible to Elisa and they had given up all hope of the Italian police ever solving the riddle. So they might have decided to take the law into their own hands, like a lynch mob.

But why give him advance notice? Why not just do it?

'Someone wants to make me sweat,' he suggested. It also gave him the chance to do exactly what he had done − alert the police. There was a possibility that the cartridges had been despatched by someone who was fanatical about Restivo's perceived guilt and this was a desperate contrivance to panic him into confessing. After all, wouldn't being locked away in prison be preferable to the prospect of an assassin's bullet? More likely, though, this was an elaborate stunt, a smokescreen, senior officers in Bournemouth surmised. It was certainly a very convenient distraction just as the hounds were snapping at the heels of their quarry.

None of the police in Bournemouth or Italy had forgotten the bogus e-mail sent to Elisa's mother, allegedly from her missing daughter. But a PI had traced its origin to a cyber café in Potenza. Was this another deception? The police suspected that it was but, of course, they were keeping an open mind.

The Salerno detectives, more so than their British

counterparts, were familiar with Mafia methods and cartridges in the post. The Dorset investigators therefore chose initially to take the threat seriously, but they were not, under any circumstances, going to be diverted from the primary investigation into Heather Barnett's murder.

The package had been posted in the Naples area. The name and address had been written in capital letters, so too the threatening note, so there was no chance of identifying the sender from handwriting. There was one certainty, however – Restivo had not posted the cartridges to himself. On the date they were mailed, Restivo was definitely in Bournemouth, although the scam, if that is what it was, could have been arranged through an intermediary.

Potenza resident Dino Seppe, said, 'You have to understand that Restivo had become a hate figure in our town. So much dirt had been written about him. We Italians are very much family people. No one in our town believed his story about what happened when he met that young girl in that beautiful church. I don't think anybody truly had any real idea what went on, except that it wasn't the way Restivo told it.

'Why would that girl have run off after such a brief encounter with him in church? She was going out with her family. All his talk about her being so unhappy was a pack of lies. I didn't know them personally, but a close friend of mine did. He told me you couldn't have met a happier girl than Elisa; always smiling and laughing, always embracing her mother and holding her hand. To say that she was talking about having to get away is wicked.'

If that prevailing attitude was true, then wasn't it likely that someone from the town had genuinely mailed the cartridges?

'It is possible,' said Tony Peppi, who had associated with

Restivo around the time he was accused of perjury. 'He was always very plausible. Very self-assured. I didn't know him at the actual time of the girl's disappearance, though.

'There was always a mysterious side to him. He liked to create what you might call an aura of mystique. He was a bit of a Walter Mitty character.'

In addition to looking into the purported threat against Restivo, Dorset detectives were on a whistle-stop tour of five Italian cities, interviewing, via an interpreter, a total of 15 women who had responded to the TV appeals for anyone to come forward who had been a victim of the mysterious public hair-cutter. The detectives returned to Bournemouth with statements and DNA samples.

All the theorising, speculation and posturing came to an abrupt end on Wednesday, 17 March 2010.

NAIL IN THE COFFIN

Spring comes early in southern Italy. The flowers are in full bloom by March, a perfect time to enjoy the beauty of the natural environment before the energy-sapping heat of the summer to come. And on Wednesday, 17 March 2010, Filomena Claps was still thinking about the planned family picnic that had had to be cancelled 17 years earlier because her daughter, Elisa, never returned from church. There was no special reason for her to be brooding about that fateful Sunday – it was something she did every day, as it had become as much a part of her life as breathing.

During the winter, a leak had developed in the roof of the Most Holy Trinity Church. Because it dated back to the 15th century, there was always some repair work or other that required attention. The rainy season had been particularly prolonged that winter, making the problem at the church worse. The constant dripping had led to puddles that the priests had to mop up daily, and the continual dampness was causing much of the ancient woodwork to rot. Consequently, workmen were called in to undertake urgent repairs, beginning on the Monday, 15 March.

On the Wednesday they arrived early in the morning, and prepared for another eight hours' arduous graft up in the roof space. The day had dawned unusually damp and chilly for the time of year, almost as if it was a portent. The leak seemed to emanate from a rooftop garret that was hard to reach; its access had been blocked, almost sealed, and quite a bit of hammering and demolition was required before the workmen were able, heads bowed, to gain entry.

The interior of the garret room was poorly lit and in need of desperate repair. But it was neither the dampness nor darkness that made a first impression on the workmen – it was the smell, a smell that was almost choking in its intensity.

'Grief!' exclaimed one of the workers, simultaneously clasping his mouth with a hand, stopping himself from vomiting.

Others clamped handkerchiefs to their mouths. 'Must be rats,' said another of the men. 'Dead rats. I've smelt it before.'

One of them had a flashlight. The beam moved from the ceiling to the walls and then the floor. An alcove in a corner appeared to have been partially bricked up and it was from that area that the vile stench was originating. Dismantling the bricks that blocked the passage to the alcove took longer than anticipated because of the cramped condition, but eventually they broke through.

And suddenly Elisa Claps had reappeared.

At the time, the workmen had no appreciation of the momentous nature of their discovery, of course. Even when the whole of Potenza was buzzing with news, the police were refusing to confirm officially that the human skeletal remains were those of Elisa Claps. But in the minds of everyone, there was no doubt.

Detectives were astonished by the fact that Elisa's clothing and accessories looked almost the same as on the day she disappeared 17 years earlier. If ever found, the police had expected nothing more than a skeleton and disintegrated clothing, especially after this amount of time. But a quirk of nature had given them a helping hand. Although the hot climate and humidity had led to decomposition of the body, it had helped to preserve everything else in pristine condition. Her hair and clothing matched perfectly the description given to the police on 12 November 1993. Her watch was still wrapped around her skeletal wrist; wire-rimmed glasses rested beside her; she was still even wearing her blue leather sandals and jewellery.

When Filomena was shown the clothes and belongings, she said, 'Yes, they're Elisa's. They're what she was wearing that Sunday.'

A little later, after an hour in church on her knees, in front of the altar in prayer, she said to her son, Gildo, 'We have our Elisa back at last. Not the way we prayed for, but at least we have her. We can have a funeral now. There will be a place where I can visit her every day; where I can sit with her; where we can talk.'

An autopsy revealed that Elisa had been battered with a large, blunt instrument, stabbed 13 times and brutally sexually assaulted. Other findings indicated that the body had been dragged by the feet and then probably rolled laterally until it occupied the space where it was eventually found; the stabbing weapon was likely to have been a single-edged knife, with a small, sharp, very strong blade; Elisa's trousers had been lowered beneath her underwear; the elastic of her knickers had snapped; her bra had broken between the cups; and the pathologist had cause to conclude that the 'fatal aggression' had occurred during 'sexual acts'.

But the most distinguishing and telling feature of all was something the Italian detectives did not make public until speaking with the Dorset investigators: a clump of hair had been cut from Elisa's head and left in one of her hands.

Was there a link between the murders of Elisa Claps and Heather Barnett? Nine years and thousands of miles separated the crimes, but they shared the remarkable feature of the grasping of strands of human hair. The Heather Barnett slaying, in all facets other than the rape, seemed a replica of the Elisa Claps crime. Could a British mother and an Italian teenager be linked through an encounter with the same man, who was now on the verge of being brought to justice?

★ ★ ★

Detectives in Dorset were naturally saddened for the family of Elisa Claps, but quietly elated, too, as the news filtered through of the gruesome find in Potenza. The collective euphoria was not an inappropriate display of disrespect for the dead; quite the reverse, in fact. This was a kneejerk outpouring of relief because now there was unbridled confidence that they were going to get their man. The 'hard yards' were now paying off, and the police cared deeply that there should be justice for Heather, Elisa and their families.

Within hours, detectives from Dorset's special squad, led by Supt Cooper who had been James's deputy, were flying back to the Italian town which had become almost their second home in recent years. Vital to them was the uncontaminated preservation of every scrap of forensic evidence. The offer still stood for the UK's unrivalled DNA laboratories to be at the Italians' disposal.

Even before the Dorset officers were airborne, surveillance on Restivo and his home in Bournemouth had been tightened. The Government's Communications Headquarters (GCHQ) at Cheltenham, a vital arm of Britain's worldwide intelligence-gathering network, had been tracking all his phone calls in and out, including those on his mobiles. They also had a record of every e-mail he had sent and received. Of special interest to the police was any communication with people in Potenza and the Naples area, particularly in relation to the threatening message to Restivo and the bullet cartridges.

From discreet intelligence-gathering, it was also apparent that Restivo was keeping himself updated on all the latest developments in his home town. Conjecture was rife among detectives assigned to the case in the UK and Italy. Some thought that Restivo's nerve would now splinter and he might well try to do a runner. But those who had interviewed him over the years believed he would remain as calm as ever – and they were right. He simply continued with his daily routine as if he hadn't a care in the world.

There was also humbling self-assurance where one might have anticipated hysteria. Bravely, Gildo's wife Irena talked to the press. 'These are not exactly the best of times for us, as you can imagine,' she said with a degree of understatement. 'It is very hard. We have been living with this for 17 years and we have been strong throughout that time and we stay strong. We really knew all along that something had happened to her, but it is devastating when you finally have to face the reality of a tragic end.'

Gildo was driving home from a business meeting in Naples when detectives in Potenza called his mobile phone to give him the news. By the time he reached Potenza, the Most Holy Trinity Church had been turned into a major crime scene and was cordoned off. He was not allowed beyond the tape, let alone inside the church.

Journalists and camera crews from all over the country were on their way and the media circus would hit town by nightfall.

The primary emotion expressed by the family was anger, which was articulated by Irena. 'The church was central to this right from the beginning. It's where we knew she was all the time. Now all we want is justice to be done, but that may be a long process, too.'

The police in the UK and Italy moved quickly and were careful to avoid any mistakes at this critical final stage. The momentum was now with them and there was a combined determination that the moment would not be missed, and that every detail was in place before making their move.

Giuseppe Persano, a spokesman for the police in Potenza, guardedly reported that the dovetailing between his troops and those in Dorset was at its peak. In Bournemouth, police statements to the media were equally circumspect. 'Dorset Police remain as resolute and committed to catching her

[Heather's] brutal killer as we were in the days and weeks after Heather's tragic death. This is an unusual murder case and the professional and focused investigation continues to be a challenge. We have been following several lines of specific, detailed and continuing inquiry. We have also been liaising closely with Interpol and the Italian police. We are utilising the latest advances in DNA genetic profiling and Dorset Police are committed to achieving justice for Heather, her two children and the rest of the family.'

The anger of the Claps family was nothing compared to the communal fury spreading like a wildfire through their town. Newspapers demanded an answer to the most pressing question: how could Elisa's body remain undetected for 17 years in the very building where she was last known to have been alive? Newspaper editor Mimmo Sammartino demanded a full-scale independent investigation.

A mass protest march and rally were hastily organised for the Saturday following the discovery. Every member of the Claps family lay a wreath in the town's main square, which was overflowing with weeping mourners.

Highlighting the collective call for transparency, a message on the town's official website read, 'Silence kills ... and we don't want to kill her twice.'

A little over two weeks later, it was the Easter weekend, traditionally a time of feasts and festivities between many Masses, but the Most Holy Trinity Church remained bolted and guarded by police sentries. For the first time in its centuries of worship, Easter was not celebrated in this historic church.

Meanwhile, in Dorset, Heather's brother Ben, a teacher, said, 'I'm just hoping that there's something they find with

Elisa's body that might lead to the killer and, hopefully, to the killer of my sister. We have had a series of episodes where there has been fresh hope and nothing has come of it. But it is an amazing discovery and could produce the clinching evidence.'

Restivo's Italian lawyer, Mario Marinelli, commented briefly, 'Danilo is in England and has been informed about the recovery of the human remains. He is quite calm about it.'

The official findings of the autopsy were not released until early in April in Bari. One of the leading Italian prosecutors said, 'We all believe something will happen very soon. Everyone is just waiting. We think that things will move quickly. It is a waiting game.'

The prospect of a legal tug-of-war now loomed, if all forensic and circumstantial evidence pointed to Restivo being the culprit. The Italians would probably feel the need to stake their claim to Restivo standing trial in Italy for Elisa's murder, emphasising that she was the earlier victim, and any other authority wishing to bring him to account would have to wait. The Dorset Police would naturally want to maintain control of Restivo, and try him for Heather's murder, arguing that he is currently residing within their jurisdiction, giving them the priority over him.

An even more contentious and subjective issue was which of the two crimes would be easier to prosecute. Forensic evidence at the scene of the crime in Bournemouth was scarce, but Heather's murder was much more recent than Elisa's and followed a series of well-documented hair-cutting incidents, which had become pertinent. Against that, more mistakes appeared to have been made in Potenza by the killer.

Each side was beginning to press its claim, in a sort of

diplomatic bidding war, although supposedly within the spirit of EU 'cooperation'. The Italians were hoping for a European arrest warrant to be issued, which would have to be executed by police in the UK and would be bound to a tight time-scale, a 48-hour period in which to present Restivo before City of Westminster magistrates in London. The decision on whether a prima-facie case against Restivo had been made would be at the discretion of a judge. If he or she was so disposed, it would be for the judge to initiate extradition proceedings, which could take months.

Meanwhile, the gathering of evidence in the rooftop garret continued, with the findings having the dual effect of positively moving the murders of Elisa Claps and Heather Barnett closer to resolution, while adding to the distress of the Claps family who had endured enough already, and who now had to suffer the pain of learning the intimate details of the last moments of their beloved Elisa's life.

A large amount of semen deposits were found within a few feet of Elisa's skeleton. The police learned that the roof area was well known in the area as a location for clandestine sexual activity. Prostitutes frequently took their clients there, sometimes while Mass was being celebrated in the church below, and there were rumours that some people in authority had known of these sordid activities for years. Used condoms were taken away, some of which dated back many years.

Of course there was widespread relief in the fact that the search for Elisa was over. But, in a sense, this was now only the beginning. The townsfolk of Potenza demanded that the clock be turned back 17 years in retrospective analysis. Elisa was last known to be alive in the Most Holy Trinity Church;

she had been with Restivo, something he admitted readily. Surely the police had completed something as basic as a thorough search?

This had never been fully explored. Elisa might have climbed steps towards the belfry for a purely innocent reason, such as curiosity, fainted and knocked herself unconscious. She could have been lying anywhere on those premises in need of urgent medical attention. So, as leaders of the community now said, the police *must* have carried out an inch-by-inch search of the church and all its peripheral structures. If not, they were obviously guilty of a significant dereliction of duty.

The police were not very forthcoming, preferring to counter with the convenient riposte that any information could be so essential to a trial that it would be prejudicial to discuss it outside of court. Of course, a lack of answers merely incited further speculation.

The police force now had its work cut out, and one way of turning the tide might be to bring a long-standing killer to justice.

-16-

CLOSING THE NET

It was 6.30am on Wednesday, 19 May 2010. The sun had risen an hour earlier. The sky was mainly clear, apart from a thin dusting of snow-white cloud, which would soon be burned away. The weather forecasters predicted a near-perfect spring day.

A few residents were already on the move, mainly those who started work early, but most of the Charminster area had yet to stir.

A fleet of police vehicles, in the style of a funeral cortège, noiselessly cruised along Chatsworth Road in Bournemouth, stopping outside a substantial, red-brick, detached house.

It was Restivo's new home since he had moved from Capstone Road, which ran parallel to Chatsworth.

Twelve detectives exited their vehicles, and car doors were closed gently. There was no overt urgency, no dawn-raid madness, no hype. If this was a defining moment, it was low-key, apart from the number of personnel involved. The handful of early risers in Chatsworth Road observed the activity in silence.

Det Supt Mark Cooper, who was now spearheading the Dorset end of the investigation, buttoned up the jacket of his grey, lightweight suit. He had a fresh, boyish face, light-brown hair and looked impossibly young for his senior rank, clearly a fast-tracker. Smartly dressed, he wore a white shirt with starched collar and a tie striped with pastel shades.

Supt Cooper silently signalled with a nod, then led the way towards Restivo's front door. His team had been well briefed; they all knew their roles. The rehearsals were over. As Supt Cooper approached the house, other officers fanned out, covering the property's rear and sides.

Not until everyone was in place did Supt Cooper rap on the front door and ring the bell. Restivo was inside, something the police already knew. Nothing had been left to chance. Restivo's movements had been monitored meticulously. They knew when he went to the bathroom, when he sneezed, when he snored. Surveillance, including electronic, had been mounted day and night.

These early-morning raids always produced stereotypical exchanges through locked front doors: 'Who is it? … What do you want? … Oh, wait a minute while I make myself decent … Hold your fire! I'm coming.'

Cooper went through the ritual of flashing his ID, before entering the house along with several other officers. There was no resistance after he informed Restivo that he was being arrested, yet again. But Restivo did protest that this was becoming 'beyond a joke' and that he considered himself a victim of police harassment.

When he emerged handcuffed, he was dressed in trainers, a grey, hooded fleece over his upper body and head, and a reddish towel covering his face. The operation was carefully choreographed, so as the car carrying Restivo away for questioning had only just swung out of Chatsworth Road, a fleet of other vehicles with the white, boiler-suited forensics team and other scene-of-crime investigators turned into the road from the other end. The occupants of all the vehicles were in constant contact by mobile, providing a running commentary.

Scaffolding was hastily erected around the house, while sheets of white tarpaulin were hoisted over the façade, up to the height of the roof, obscuring all views from the road of activity within the building. All areas of the garden were dug up and lorry-loads of materials were driven away during the next few days.

Shortly before these developments, Cooper had told Bournemouth's *Daily Echo* newspaper, 'All the focus and attention has been on Italy in the past two months, but there has been a huge amount of activity here in the UK. Things have been moving very fast as far as our own investigation is concerned and I believe we are very close to a breakthrough.' He was not over-playing his hand.

Professional observers were divided over their prognosis of the outcome. After all, Restivo had already been arrested twice previously by Dorset Police and released without charge both times. In Italy, he had been interrogated endlessly and, although imprisoned for a while for perjury, he had not been arraigned for murder.

This time however, there was a big difference from the other arrests. The discovery of Elisa Claps's remains and the hair in her hand had created a link between the two crimes which demanded further investigation.

One more thing – and known at that stage only to the investigators in Italy and Britain – some blood on Elisa's clothing had matched Restivo's DNA. The blood could not have come from a cut made when he claimed to have fallen on a building site in the afternoon because that would have been *after* the murder. How else could the blood could have been deposited, other than as a result of Elisa fighting for her life?

For a number of years, investigators in the UK and Italy were certain that Restivo was their man. But had they now sufficient evidence to make it stick? Had Elisa Claps's skeletal remains made enough of a difference? And if yes, who held the stronger hand – the UK or Italy? There were sceptics in the international press corps and among veteran police officers who believed that, despite the mounting evidence, he'd manage to wriggle free, yet again.

They were wrong, of course, because they were not privy to the latest incriminating evidence.

★ ★ ★

In the afternoon of the day following his latest arrest, Danilo Restivo was charged at Poole Police Station with the murder of Heather Barnett. The Dorset investigators had pre-empted the Italian bid for staging the first instalment of this epic.

Insiders were to say that he reacted with arrogant disbelief. 'He was truly flabbergasted. He acted as if Cooper and other detectives were off their trolleys. Everything about his body language was derisive. His attitude was one of "we've been through all this before".'

News of this dramatic development by the police was released outside the police station in Poole by Alastair Nisbet of the Crown Prosecution Service, accompanied by Supt Cooper.

'After carefully considering all the evidence provided to me by Dorset Police, arising from their investigation into the murder of Heather Barnett in November 2002, I have decided that there is sufficient evidence to prosecute Danilo Restivo for her murder and that it would be in the public interest to do so,' said Nisbet.

'Accordingly, I have authorised the police to charge him with that offence and he will appear at Bournemouth Magistrates' Court.

'The family of Heather Barnett have been informed of my decision and I hope soon to be able to meet them to explain the trial process and answer any questions they have.'

Cooper, obviously on a high, also made a statement. 'I would like to say a few words about bringing the Heather Barnett murder investigation to the critical point it has reached today.

'Danilo Restivo has been in custody for the last 35 hours and has been interviewed at length. We have presented details of that interview, as well as evidence gathered over the past seven-and-a-half years, to the Crown Prosecution Service.

'The progression of the investigation to this point today demonstrates the professionalism, commitment and tireless work of those Dorset Police officers involved in Heather's case. You'll appreciate we can't go into any further detail.

'We have been in close contact with members of Heather's family throughout the course of this investigation, including speaking with them this morning to make them aware of the charges brought against Restivo.

'This family has shown extraordinary strength and courage over the seven years since Heather's death and our thoughts are still very much with them.

'Heather's case is now in the hands of our partners in the criminal justice system and we will continue to work closely with them.'

After appearing before Bournemouth magistrates the following day, Restivo was further remanded in custody until 24 September, when the case would be passed for review and assessment to Winchester Crown Court.

Although at this stage Restivo was already being legally represented by Tracey Watson, a solicitor with the Bournemouth firm Jacobs and Reeves, he boasted in prison that the world's most celebrated lawyer would be taking up his case because they were blood brothers; by that, he meant they were both Italian. Of course, he was referring to Giovanni di Stefano, 'The Devil's Advocate'. Such a boast, ultimately, would only serve to undermine his claims of innocence and the 'weakness' of the allegations. Di Stefano, as we've seen, specialised in hopeless cases. So is that how Restivo really saw himself now – a hopeless case? Interesting. Even more interesting considering that di Stefano was already acting for Omar Benguit, who had been sentenced to life for the murder in Bournemouth of South Korean student Jang-Ok Shin

(Oki). As far as self-publicity went, Restivo had possibly scored a spectacular own goal.

Meanwhile, in Salerno, Chief Prosecutor Franco Roberti and his deputy, Rosa Volpe, applied for a time-limited extradition of Restivo from the UK to enable them to question him in front of a judge and probably charge him with murdering Elisa Claps. The application was to be made through Britain's Serious Organised Crime Agency (SOCA). However, now that Restivo had been charged in Britain and was officially part of the legal process, one that led inexorably towards trial, the UK prosecutors were adamant that the only journeys he'd be making in the near future would be the commute between prison and court in England.

On Monday, 8 November 2010, speaking in Italian through an interpreter, Restivo pleaded not guilty at Winchester Crown Court to the murder of Heather Barnett. The preliminary hearing, presided over by Judge Keith Cutler, lasted a mere 20 minutes. Restivo was dressed smartly in a grey suit and striped tie. His dark hair was receding at the front and sides, but was full and slightly curled at the back. He held himself ramrod straight with his chest puffed out. He coolly stared back at the judge through rimless glasses. His pink, plump cheeks and double chin were clean-shaven. Throughout his 20 minutes in court, he affected the air of a respectable and confident professional. His barrister, David Jeremy QC, made no application for bail.

The judge settled on 4 May 2011 for the start of the trial, putting aside at least two months for its duration. He said that it could have begun earlier, but would probably have been suspended for the Easter period and he was anxious to maintain as much continuity as possible for the jury in what was going to be a very complex case.

The stage was at last set for what the legal experts were predicting would be one of the most riveting murder trials in recent British legal history.

OUT OF THEIR MINDS

I t goes without saying that every serial killer begins with a tally of one. Some would-be serial killers are caught after their first crime. Obviously, though, they are still warped with the perverted psyche of a serial killer. No one better understands this uniquely evil species better than Dr Helen Morrison, MD, a forensic psychiatrist in the USA who has spent more than 400 hours alone with the world's most callous serial killers. Her research has revolutionised the profiling of depraved men and women whom sane people believe murder randomly and without motive.

Dr Morrison, who lives in Chicago with her children and neurosurgeon husband, has been attributed with pushing back the frontiers of psychiatric research into thrill-seeking murderers who kill on a grand scale pitilessly and calculatingly.

So much can be learned from her experiences, which she has written and lectured about. She writes:

My job is grounded in careful science and in reasoned theory. After speaking at length to more than 80 of them, I have found that serial murderers do not relate to others on any level that you would expect one person to relate to another. They can play roles beautifully, create complex, earnest performances to which no Hollywood Oscar winner could hold a candle. They can mimic anything. They can appear to be complete and whole human beings and, in some cases, are seen to be pillars of society. But they're missing a very essential core of human relatedness. For them, killing is nothing; nothing at all. Serial murderers have no emotional connection to their victims. That's probably the most chilling part of it. Not only do they not care, but they also have no ability to care.

With serial killers, I never quite know whom I'm dealing with. They are so friendly and so kind and very solicitous at the beginning of our work together. I've been swept up into their world, and that world, however briefly, can seem right. I've often thought: is this person the right person? Is all the work I've done — painstaking research, scientific collection of data, complex theorising — simply wrong? Maybe I missed something. They're charming, almost unbelievably so, charismatic, like a Cary Grant or a George Clooney. They treat me as if I am their kindred spirit.

However, when I sit with them for four to six hours at a time, solid, without interruption, everything changes. My interviews are crafted to seem like talks, easy conversations. I've learned that a serial murderer can't maintain his solicitous role for any period of time past two to three hours. At this point I can begin to strip away the superficial layer of affability to reveal a dark, barren core.

What triggers their actions? What makes them tick? Why do they continually hunger for murder? The popular perception is that they have been physically and/or sexually abused by their parents when they were innocent children.

Yorkshire Ripper Peter Sutcliffe, while working as a grave digger, heard voices that to him were an experience as profound as the burning bush to Moses, according to Dr Morrison.

This was how Sutcliffe described his moment of revelation: 'I felt it was very wonderful at the time. I heard what I believed then and believe now to be God's voice. It was starting to rain. I remember going to the top of a slope overlooking the valley and I felt as though I had just experienced something fantastic. I looked across the valley and all around and thought of Heaven and Earth and how insignificant we all were. But I felt so important at that moment.'

Hearing religious voices and dancing to their tunes is common among those who kill without any rational motive. In her book, *My Life Among the Serial Killers* (John Wiley and Sons Ltd), Dr Morrison reminds readers:

Jeffrey Dahmer, who had sex with his dead victims and ate parts of their bodies, built a kind of altar to both God and Satan in his apartment. It was a gruesome sanctum that included skulls of his victims in which he would burn incense so that he might absorb special powers and energies.

Joseph Kallinger – who in addition to committing other

murders, also drowned his son Joey with the aid of another son, Mike – stated that he was also on a divine mission from God. When these killers hear voices from God, what they're really hearing is only their own inner voice, imagined permutations of what's in their own minds. They may want to have someone else to blame for their inhuman deeds or they may want to feel more important than they really are, as if they are angels of God sent to earth to scrub it clean from its immoral filth.

In the case of Sutcliffe, the comments that he saw 'how insignificant we all were' and that 'I felt so important at that moment' make me think once again that, like other serial killers, he was emotionally a very young child. Who, other than an infant, feels that he is controlling not just the world but the universe around him? Who else but an infant feels so important that he thinks he is the centre of the universe? And who else but a child would think in this way for no particular reason, not for wealth, not for power, not for human domination, but just to maintain and protect his own personal cosmos?

Sutcliffe indeed felt that he had been chosen. As the months began to pass, the voice, which had been initially comforting, suggested to Peter that he becomes violent.

Of the voice, Sutcliffe explained, 'It kept saying that I had to go on a mission to remove prostitutes, to get rid of them.'

Generations have been brainwashed into believing that 'recreational' serial killing began with Jack the Ripper. Not so. For example, Baron Gilles de Rais, a war hero ally of Joan of Arc, was killing for kicks in France in the 1400s. He was handsome, rich and amassed a huge collection of castles.

One of these edifices, forbidding and turreted on the outskirts of the French village of Machecoul, was the epicentre of his debauched criminality. Daily, his servants were despatched on child-snatching missions.

On 11 October 1442, he was charged with murdering 140 young children. After being found guilty he was hanged on 26 October, after which his body was burned.

The first murder had been committed shortly after the death of his grandfather, who had been a surrogate parent to him, albeit an abusive one. De Rais's parents had died when he was 11, something of significance to Dr Morrison. The death of a close relative can be one of the triggers to serial killing, she has suggested. 'Like other serial killers after him, de Rais chose to kill the marginal in society, those that were easily attainable.'

Heather Barnett, a lone parent working from home and anxious to make ends meet, was easily attainable. So, too, Elisa Claps, an impressionable teenager who had a head dizzy with romantic dreams. And not long before Elisa was murdered, Restivo had been rocked by the death of a relative.

'Cold-blooded' killer has become such a cliché that its impact is diminished. Much more graphic and chilling than labels are first-hand accounts by multiple murderers, but these are rare because most serial killers are either in denial or too arrogant to deign to explain themselves to ordinary, normal people who simply wouldn't understand their hyper-creative thought processes.

Dr Morrison had criticised what she calls 'territorial protectionism' throughout the world of law enforcement agencies. 'They don't want anyone messing around or flying in to add new ideas or theories,' she said. 'And they don't want anyone else getting credit for the capture except themselves. Additionally, they don't understand how sitting and talking something through might be helpful.'

The Italians were very insular and introspective for several years over Elisa Claps's disappearance, rejecting offers of assistance from Rome and Salerno, let alone the UK and the USA's FBI, insisting that the case was a local problem. It was not until Gildo, Elisa's brother, became the conduit, forging a link between the police from his region of Italy and the Dorset force, that barriers began to be torn down and a constructive working relationship grew. Even then, there was possessiveness over gathered evidence and a distinct caginess over sharing leads. And the relationship was done no favours when it came to the race to trial, and the question of who should take responsibility to try Restivo first. Possession it seems, even when bringing an alleged killer to trial, is nine-tenths of the law.

The Italians, incidentally, were also seriously hampered by several blind alleys and wild-goose chases on their way to finding Elisa Claps's whereabouts, and then her killer. One such example was the confusion surrounding a discovery after a fire in Rome in 2007, in which human remains were found to be present. Indeed, a human skull was unearthed, and then other bones, which formed a rather unusual human skeleton – unusual because it turned out to be made up of bones from five different individuals – three women and two men.

At the time, Italy did not have a national DNA database, so there were immediate obstacles to identification. Could one of these victims be Elisa Claps? And who on earth were the others? And was there a serial killer on the loose who had a penchant for rearranging bones? The police were baffled, and unable to find sufficient evidence to identify these victims, or piece together the circumstances surrounding their deaths. And not until Elisa's remains came to light in 2010 was she eliminated from the mystery. At the time of writing, the police in Rome had still not identified any of the five people whose bones had been used to build the 'jigsaw skeleton'.

Through her research, Dr Morrison identifies these nine similarities that she feels are common to all serial killers:

- They do not have motives for their murders
- They have no personality structures and do not fit into the usual theories of development espoused by people like Freud or Kohut
- They are not psychopaths, who have the ability to control what they do, think and feel
- They are not mentally retarded; most of them have above-average intelligence
- They are not psychologically complete human beings, even though they can mimic and play roles
- They have not all been sexually or physically abused
- They are addicted to killing and they cannot control their actions
- Serial murder is not a phenomenon of only Western society; it is universal
- There is nothing new about serial killing; it probably began thousands of years ago

It would now be up to a trial jury to determine Restivo's involvement in the murders of Heather Barnett and Elisa Claps.

-18-

TRIED AND TESTED

The trial of Danilo Restivo began in Court Number Two at Winchester Crown Court on Wednesday, 11 May 2011, with the Honourable Mr Justice Burnett presiding. As Sir Ian Burnett QC, in 2007–08, he was lead counsel to the coroner on behalf of the Government in the Princess Diana inquest. Since then, he had been elevated to being the most senior judge on the South-West circuit.

Restivo, aged 39 by the start of his trial, wore a smart blue suit, light-blue shirt, striped tie and silver-rimmed spectacles. His raven-black hair, receding at the front, was combed back severely and appeared to have been waxed. His fleshy face sagged and his paunch put considerable pressure on the front of his shirt; it seemed unlikely that his suit jacket could be done up. He spoke only once during the entire first day and that was to confirm his name. At all times, he was flanked in the dock by three security guards.

Mr Michael Bowes QC, a formidable prosecutor with an impressive international reputation, led for the Crown. He had made a name for himself successfully prosecuting insider dealers and advised legal teams in the Middle East and New York.

Leading the defence was David Jeremy QC, who, earlier in 2011, secured the acquittal of horse-trainer Kirsti Windsor, aged 38, who had been accused of killing her former boyfriend and burning his body on a bonfire while she watched and drank wine. After a six-week trial, the jury was unanimous in its 'not guilty' verdict.

And in 2009, Mr Jeremy defended one of three defendants accused of 'murder by execution' on a London street. His exposure of technical failings by the prosecution over the advanced disclosure of evidence involving alleged, incriminating, prison-cell confessions led to the acquittal of all three defendants.

The whole of the first morning was monopolised by legal arguments before the jury selection process could commence. Every word spoken in court was translated into Italian by official interpreter Valerie Malandra for Restivo's benefit.

The judge then spent some time explaining to the foreign media the finer points of British legislation in respect of court reporting. TV crews were present from Italy and the USA. Journalists from many countries spilled over from the press benches in the bowl of the court to the upstairs public gallery. The judge emphasised that nothing could be reported during the trial of anything that was debated in the absence of the jury. This included the legal arguments of that morning. Some of the crews had expected to be able to set up their cameras and microphones in court.

While awaiting trial, Restivo had been transferred to Belmarsh Prison in south-east London, a relatively new establishment, opened in 1991 on part of the former Royal Arsenal in Woolwich and adjacent to the local Crown Court. Between 2001–02 it became known as Britain's Guantanamo Bay because prisoners were detained there indefinitely without charge or trial under provisions of the Anti-Terrorism Act. Although this was reversed by the Law Lords on the grounds of discrimination against the Human Rights Act, the prison continued to be used for terrorist-related offences and offenders who were believed to pose a risk to national security or thought to be potential escapees. In 2009, Her Majesty's Chief Inspector of Prisons criticised the 'extremely high amount of force' used to control inmates.

The judge, however, balked at the idea of Restivo being ferried backwards and forwards between Belmarsh and Winchester, a very long journey, if for no other reason than the problems it would present the defence team with daily briefings. Consequently, it was arranged for Restivo to be kept in Winchester Prison from Monday to Friday and returned to Belmarsh for weekends.

Selecting a jury did not begin until the afternoon of the first day. The task of selecting 12 from a pool of 64 was a protracted one, almost USA-style, as over a number of days each one was grilled about his or her knowledge of the case and any possible prejudices. The trial proper did not begin until the following Monday before a jury comprising seven men and five women.

The public gallery was full when Mr Bowes opened the case for the prosecution. Among the members of the public in court was Elisa Claps's mother, Filomena.

'Heather Barnett was murdered on 12 November 2002 and it is the prosecution's case that she was murdered by Danilo Restivo,' Mr Bowes began, his delivery low-key and easy on the ear. No theatrics, no great drama, the approach very much that the facts would do all the talking.

Danilo Restivo has denied murdering Heather Barnett and denied being present in her house on 12 November 2002. The central issue in the case is, therefore, the identity of the murderer.

In addition to evidence from the scene of the murder and other surrounding circumstances, the prosecution's case is that Danilo Restivo's conduct on other occasions also proves that he was the person who murdered Heather Barnett.

There were certain striking features in relation to the circumstances of Heather Barnett's murder which may be summarised as follows: (i) Heather Barnett was found with a clump of hair belonging to another person in her right hand; (ii) she had hair below her left hand which had been cut from her head with a knife; (iii) her trousers had been lowered, exposing her pants and pubic hair; (iv) her bra had been broken or cut from the front; (v) it is the prosecution's case that Heather Barnett's murder was premeditated and that her killer was wearing gloves and changed his trousers at the scene in order to avoid forensic contamination.

It is highly likely that he was also wearing some form of over-clothing in order to protect himself further from forensic contamination and that he brought with him the blunt instrument used to kill her and the knife used to mutilate her and cut her hair.

There is very strong evidence from a substantial number of women and girls, both in England and in Italy, that Danilo Restivo has sat behind them on buses or in one case in the cinema and surreptitiously cut their hair without their consent. It is very clear that Danilo Restivo has a propensity, or fetish, for cutting hair from women without their consent. It is understood that he admits this conduct, both in Italy and in England, and you will hear evidence about it during the trial.

The prosecution's case is that this evidence is highly probative in establishing that it was Danilo Restivo who murdered Heather Barnett, leaving someone else's hair in her right hand and cutting her own hair from her after death and leaving it under her left hand.

Mr Bowes then outlined police observations of Restivo during April and May in 2004 at secluded locations near Bournemouth, namely Throop Mill and Pig Shoot Lane, where his behaviour was considered suspicious:

Despite the relatively warm weather, he was observed at different times to change jackets, put on over-trousers and gloves, and change his trainers. He appeared to be observing women in the area and on a number of occasions appeared to be following certain women. On several occasions, he had a black bag with him.

On 12 May, he was observed at Throop Mill wearing a pair of dark over-trousers and a dark coat. He had gloves with him and was carrying the same shoulder-bag as had been seen with him on 6 May. He returned to his car and placed the bag

*in the back of the car. He was then approached by uniformed
officers who asked him what he had been doing and he said
he had been walking for exercise.*

*The officers began to search the car and asked whether
there was anything sharp or dangerous in it. Danilo Restivo
replied, "There's a knife in the bag in the back." The police
searched the holdall and found it contained only a large
fillet-type knife and a packet of tissues. In the boot, the police
found a hooded jacket which contained a balaclava in the
front pocket and a pair of gloves in the side pockets. Two
pairs of scissors were recovered from the driver's door-pocket
of the car.*

*It is the prosecution's case that the evidence of him showing
an interest in and/or following women, when wearing this
type of over-clothing and carrying a bag containing nothing
but a large, sharp knife and some tissue, forms parts of a
cumulative picture which establishes him as the person who
killed Heather Barnett.*

Police Constable Ian Fryett told the court that the knife was
found while searching Restivo's white Metro car. Restivo
was 'sweating profusely' when approached; so much so that
the sweat was dripping from his nose and face.

The jury was shown the video footage which included
clips of Restivo pulling a dark coat over his head so that only
his nose and glasses could be seen. The gist of the
prosecution case was that Restivo was out hunting women,
preparing to stalk, with scissors ready for clipping hair and a
gruesome knife at hand for a more serious assault, should the
opportunity present itself.

The prosecution will present evidence that on 12 September 1993, Danilo Restivo murdered a young girl called Elisa Claps whom he knew and whom he had arranged to meet that day at the Church of the Most Holy Trinity in Potenza, Italy.

After their meeting, she was not seen again. Her body was only discovered in a loft at the top of the church on 17 March 2010, where it had lain since her disappearance on 12 September 1993.

Elisa Claps received multiple stab wounds and a post mortem examination has revealed a number of striking similarities between her murder and the murder of Heather Barnett. In particular, next to her body there were locks of her own hair which had been cut from her head shortly after death.

In addition, Elisa Claps' trousers and pants were lowered to the same level as of those of Heather Barnett and Elisa Claps' bra was cut or broken at the front, in the same way as Heather Barnett's bra was cut or broken at the front.

Danilo Restivo has not yet been tried in Italy for the murder of Elisa Claps and you will not be asked to return a verdict in relation to that allegation. You could not be asked to return any verdict in relation to the murder of Elisa Claps as, under the law in this country, there is no jurisdiction to try a foreign national for an alleged murder committed abroad.

An inquiry into the disappearance and death of Elisa Claps has been taking place in Italy and some of that evidence will be called before you by the prosecution in this case. It is important that you understand at the outset of the case the reason why this evidence is being put before you and why the prosecution says that it is powerful evidence in proving that Danilo Restivo was the person who murdered Heather Barnett.

There is compelling evidence to prove that Danilo Restivo murdered Elisa Claps. The presence of cut hair after death in both cases, together with the other features relating to the clothing of both victims, is strikingly similar and as akin to a hallmark.

The prosecution's case is that the circumstances in which Elisa Claps was killed so closely resemble the circumstances in which Heather Barnett was killed that you can have no doubt that both of the killings must have been the work of one person. That is Danilo Restivo.

Mr Bowes told the jury that Restivo had a conviction in Italy for perjury relating to the disappearance of Elisa Claps. 'On 7 March 1995, Danilo Restivo was convicted by the Potenza Criminal Court of giving false information to the prosecutor in relation to his account of an injury to his hand, sustained on 12 September 1993,' said Mr Bowes. 'The prosecution's contention is that Danilo Restivo lied in the way he described [the way he injured his hand] in order to conceal the fact that he had killed Elisa Claps. However, this conviction is relevant also to the issue of the defendant's credibility and the prosecution's contention is that it shows a propensity to be untruthful.'

Referring to the killer's clothing on the day of the crime, Mr Bowes outlined the reasons why the murder had been premeditated. The murderer had a second pair of trainers with him to change into after the attack, he alleged. 'It is highly likely that the killer was also wearing some form of over-clothing and had with him the blunt instrument used to kill Heather Barnett,' he continued. 'And the knife used to mutilate her and cut her hair after death.

'The pattern of footprints developed in Luminol and the absence of footprints in the hallway up to the front door supports the conclusion that the killer had a second pair of trainers with him. The pattern is consistent with the killer leaving the bathroom, walking up as far as the work-table in the sewing room, changing his trainers and then leaving the flat by the front door.

'In order to change trainers, the killer must have stepped on the carpet by the work-table, either in socks or in bare feet. This would have provided the opportunity for blood to be transferred from the carpet to the inside of the second pair of trainers.'

Of the trainers seized from Restivo's home by Detective Sergeant Browning, he contended that these were the shoes he put on after the murder. 'During the process of changing trainers, Danilo Restivo came into contact with blood on the carpet and transferred this into that second pair,' he said. 'Fearing that they might be seized by the police and subjected to forensic analysis, he soaked them in bleach in an attempt to destroy any forensic link.

'On 24 June 2004, Danilo Restivo was interviewed under caution about a number of matters, including the trainers found soaking in bleach. He had a solicitor present and the services of an interpreter. He accepted that they [the trainers] had been in disinfectant, but said he had decided to wash them that day because they smelt horrible due to the plastic.'

Restivo was interrogated again on 19 May 2010 about the LCV findings. He was asked to explain how bloodstains got inside his trainers. 'He made no comment,' said Mr Bowes.

Dealing with the hair-cutting fetish, Mr Bowes gave a series of examples.

On an unknown date in 2002, Tessa Cox was travelling on a bus from Bournemouth to the Throop area. She sat at the back of the bus and saw a male passenger leaning towards a female passenger and using a pair of scissors to cut her hair. The male saw Tessa Cox, concealed the scissors, and got up to leave the bus. He got off in Charminster Road, near Cemetery Junction, perhaps half a mile from Danilo Restivo's home.

The girl whose hair had been cut did not want to make a complaint and the matter was not reported to the police.

On 7 February 2008, Tessa Cox was working at Bournemouth Hospital. She was walking through Ward 12 and passed Bay 3. She saw the man in Bed 5 who had been cutting the girl's hair in 2002. She was so sure it was him that she called the police. The name on the wipe-board for the unit was 'Restivo'. The medical notes confirm that he was a patient at the hospital that day.

In December 2002, Sonia Taylor was travelling on the number 31 bus from the centre of Bournemouth to the Throop area. A man was asking for change from a £10-note in an unusual voice, perhaps foreign. She noticed her hair being pulled and saw that some of the strands were loose. The male got up hurriedly and left the bus near Cemetery Junction. She discovered her hair had been cut.

In 2006, Sonia Taylor was shown a picture of Danilo Restivo by a friend who knew of the hair-cutting incident. Sonia Taylor's reaction was that she could say "100 per cent that this was the man who cut my hair on the bus".

At about 9.00am on a day between September 2002 and May 2003, Katie McGoldrick boarded a bus on her way to school from the Triangle area of Bournemouth (central). Katie was aware of a male who got on the bus and sat directly behind her. She described the man as 25 – 30, with short, dark hair, as if he was Arabic or Italian.

Shortly into the journey, she felt a tugging sensation on her hair. She said it was gentle but felt as though it was being pulled. She shook her hair free and saw the man's face very close to the back of her head. She heard the sound of snipping. The man got off the bus at the Richmond Arms public house bus-stop, a few hundred yards from Restivo's address. When Katie got to school, she realised that her hair had been cut.

On 24 June 2004, Katie attended an identification procedure at Bournemouth Police Station and identified Restivo as the man who had sat behind her on the day her hair was cut.

At about 7.55am on 13 March 2003, Holly Stroud boarded a number 17 bus from a stop outside the Richmond Arms in Charminster Road. During her journey, she felt a tugging sensation at her hair from behind, one of those tugs was of such force that she realised it was not an accident and turned to see a man in his thirties with dark, possibly black, hair and a large forehead.

But it was not until she reached school that she discovered her hair had been cut.

On 24 June 2004, Holly identified Danilo Restivo as the man who had been sitting behind her on the bus and snipped her hair.

Mr Bowes also told the court that there was evidence from nine women in Italy that their hair had been cut off by Danilo Restivo in Potenza and Rimini.

In 1992, a young woman called Angela Campochiaro, then 23 years old, was at the cinema Ariston in Potenza, with her fiancé, now her husband, Nicola Marino. They were sitting in a row occupied only by them. During the film, Angela realised that there was someone in the seat immediately behind her and that he was touching her hair.

Angela had very long hair. The contact happened a few times, so she turned around. She then felt distinctly that the person grabbed hold of her hair. She told her fiancé what was happening.

He [Marino] looked around and, right at that moment, the first part of the film was ending and the lights went on. He saw a young man who had a jeans-jacket over his lap, which had just shifted, and he was able to see his private parts, which made him realise that the young man had been masturbating.

He recognised the young man as Danilo Restivo as he knew him and his family, and he told him to move away.

After Angela and Nicola left the cinema, they realised that Danilo Restivo had cut a lock, about 10cm long, from her hair.

When interviewed by the police on 22 June 2004, Restivo was told about the allegations made by a number of the victims of his hair-cutting in Bournemouth. He denied repeatedly that he had ever cut anybody's hair in this way.

After Restivo's arrest on 21 November 2006, the police searched the house at 93, Capstone Road. In the bedroom, which Restivo shared with Fiamma, was a Tesco bag on the floor, next to a chest of drawers. Inside the bag was a lock of hair, tied with green cotton.

When questioned about the hair in the Tesco bag, Restivo denied that it had anything to do with him. He claimed never to have seen the hair before.

His explanation was that the hair must have been 'planted' in his room, by 'a person or persons who must have gone to his house with a set of keys,' said Mr Bowes. 'He said that during the summer some keys were lost and that "my wife had copies made. I can't really remember for who. These copies could still be in circulation and be used by someone else."

'He went on to say, "We've had problems in Italy with the Claps case. I can't prove anything, what I say, but perhaps there is a connection with people to do with Claps who have put the lock of hair there. There are people who want my death, from the Claps family."'

Mr Bowes then focused on the covert electronic surveillance that had been carried out at Restivo's residence on 2 November 2006, which followed a recent screening of the popular BBC *Crimewatch* programme. This part of the recorded dialogue was read to the jury and a typed transcript given to them to study:

Fiamma (F): Anyway, definitely according to what they said last night the hair was cut some, about four weeks ago.
Restivo (R): Eh.
F: Eh, but you go on the bus then, how long is it that you do not go on the bus?
R: A long time.
F: Someone who has not, someone said that somebody cut her hair, no doubts [inaudible] she then spoke last night, the little girl going to school with her uniform.
R: Mm.
F: You cut her hair, eh? How do you mean 'Mm'? How can you go 'Mm'?
R: I don't remember.

F: If you don't remember, it means yes.
R: If I don't remember, I don't remember.
F: No, Danilo, 'Mm' means yes.
R: All right, it could be yes, it could be no.
F: I am not the police, Danilo, OK.
R: Eh?
F: I am not the police, no, OK?
R: But I am saying that I do not remember. I honestly do not remember.

[More monitoring of Restivo's premises took place on 21 November 2006. The conversation between Restivo and Fiamma went as follows:]

R: They found a lock of hair in a bag [inaudible] and they believe I cut it off. I told them that I [inaudible] can get into the house through the window and this summer the keys were lost. I did not cut those, that hair and I am prepared to do a DNA for traces, traces of possible DNA. That hair I have never seen and I have never touched it.
F: When on earth did we lose the house keys? What the fuck are you talking about?
R: The keys to the house were lost by the students.
F: Ah, yes.
R: And you asked Alex [her son] or you had the keys cut.
F: Yes.

[And on yet another occasion, the two were recorded saying, in connection with Restivo's hair-cutting fetish:]
R: I had problems [inaudible] … because I realised that …
F: I do know.

R: You knew.

F: Understood because you …

R: Eh! Don't change.

F: Because you shouldn't have done certain things. Why did you do certain things? That is what I do not get. You have seen the load of problems it has brought us in Italy. Why did you do it? You should have told me. If you hadn't done these things [inaudible] you would not be in the shit like this now.

R: Yes, I know, but I have psychological problems.

F: Ah, yes, eh. Then later we see a psychologist.

R: But I have seen him already in Italy.

F: And what did he tell you?

R: That there is nothing to worry about.

F: We shall see.

R: Eh?

F: We cannot know.

R: He did not tell me we can't know.

F: And what do you reckon I should do?

R: Aah, boh … I [inaudible] everything.

F: Everything? How? Causing harm to a person?

R: No, like … touch the hair, hold them in the hand, but then everything is visible, everything.

In her evidence to the court, forensic scientist Claire Stangoe spoke about the green towel in Heather Barnett's flat that had featured so strongly among articles taken away for examination and testing. She said that the odds of the skin flakes lifted from the towel having come from anyone other than Restivo were 57,000:1.

Mr Peter Lamb, another forensic scientist, who examined hair taken from under Heather's left hand, said that the strands had been severed near the root with a single-bladed weapon, not as sharp as a scalpel, but something like a new kitchen knife.

Restivo's alibi for the morning of the murder had been blown apart, according to prosecutor Mr Bowes. The fact that he bought a bus ticket at 8.44am proved nothing more than that, he argued. Restivo could easily have alighted at the next stop and walked back in a matter in minutes, he said. There was absolutely no evidence that he remained on the bus, but plenty to the contrary.

'We say he was back at Heather's by 8.55am, murdered and mutilated her, changed clothes and was back on Charminster Road by 9.24am,' he said. In fact, a witness would testify that Restivo was seen crossing Charminster Road at 9.24am, rather than being on his course at NACRO, about two miles away, in Wallisdown Road, just over the boundary towards Poole.

In an interview with police, Restivo claimed that he had arrived for his course at 9.00am and had immediately logged on at his computer. But, said Mr Bowes, Restivo's computer had not been used until 10.10am. 'What did or did not happen on the computer is absolutely critical to his alibi,' he continued. 'Analysis of the computer's hard-drive completely destroys Restivo's version of events as to when he used it.' He had, in fact, not arrived at NACRO until just before 10.10am.

Craig Wilson, a computer forensics specialist, confirmed that an administrator at NACRO had logged on Restivo's computer at 9.09am and there was no evidence of it being used after that until 10.10am. Mr Wilson was managing director of Digital Detective Group, a company with a global reputation that even undertook investigations for the FBI.

'I drew on all the computer data to draw up a timeline of all the activity on that computer that day,' he told the court. He had detected fragments on the hard drive of deleted stories from the Bournemouth *Daily Echo* newspaper and had pieced them back together. All those deleted stories had been coverage of Heather Barnett's murder.

Challenging Mr Wilson's evidence, Restivo's counsel, Mr Jeremy, said, 'There is a difference between no user activity and no evidence of user activity. You can only speak about the evidence you found, not the evidence that may have been there once but was subsequently deleted or overwritten. It follows you cannot be sure you recovered all the data that day.'

Mr Wilson countered, 'You would expect to find some trace of user activity if there had been any. There was no evidence and my conclusion was the computer was idle.'

Claire George, who worked in a pharmacy in Charminster Road, watched the *Crimewatch* programme on 12 September 2006. During the programme, CCTV footage was screened, showing a man crossing Charminster Road at 9.24am. She explained to the court that both Restivo and Heather Barnett were regular customers. And when she saw the figure being selected for identification on *Crimewatch*, she instantly recognised the man as Restivo.

Mr Bowes quizzed her about what made her so sure. 'The posture,' she replied. 'If you see someone enough times, you can recognise them by their posture.'

Defence counsel Mr Jeremy asked Mrs George if she might have been influenced by the fact that she knew

Restivo had previously been arrested in connection with Heather's murder and that she had considerable background knowledge of the case from newspapers and her own research on the Internet.

'No, I don't,' she answered emphatically.

Retired police officer Anthony Merrifield had recorded walking times from bus-stops at which Restivo might have alighted before reaching the NACRO building. Walking steadily, not hurrying, the longest was 11 minutes, which would have put Restivo on Heather's doorstep at 8.55am.

Unquestionably, Elisa Claps was Restivo's Achilles heel, something which Mr Bowes exploited ruthlessly:

The evidence establishes that Elisa Claps met Danilo Restivo at the church on 12 September 1993 at approximately 11.30am. She [Elisa] was due to have met her friend, Eliana De Cillis, about 15 minutes later, but never appeared.

She [Elisa] was murdered either in, or close to, the loft above the church, where her body remained without being moved until it was discovered on 17 March 2010. Danilo Restivo admitted having sexual feelings for Elisa Claps, but said she did not reciprocate them.

There is evidence that Elisa Claps was sexually assaulted. A quantity of her hair was cut from her head after her death. There is evidence of earlier incidents in Italy where Danilo Restivo cut hair from girls covertly and therefore without their consent. Danilo Restivo had a suspicious wound on his hand that afternoon and there is evidence to establish that his account of how it occurred is untrue.

For Danilo Restivo not to be responsible, it would mean

*that Elisa Claps left the church at about 11.50am, failed to
meet her friend Eliana very close by, went with another person
back to the church and up to the loft a short time afterwards
and was killed by that other person, who coincidentally also
had a fetish for cutting off women's hair.*

On the ninth day of the trial, the jurors were taken by coach
from the Winchester court to Bournemouth, a 55-minute
drive. They spent 20 minutes in the flat that had been the
home of Heather Barnett and her children. They inspected
the bathroom where the mutilated body had been left. They
saw the workroom, where Heather probably received the
fatal blows to her head.

After leaving the crime scene, they were shown the house
across the road, where Restivo had been living with
Fiamma. From there, they followed the bus route to the
NACRO training centre. It is hard to imagine a more
morbid and macabre mystery tour. The jurors were joined
by the judge, counsels for the prosecution and defence, and
other court officials. As they followed in the footsteps of
Heather, her killer and those two poor children, the horror
of the events that day so many years ago was all too obvious,
and was etched in the expressions on the faces of all the
visitors to number 112 Capstone Road.

The third week of the trial began with evidence from
Italian witnesses via a 'live' video link from a courtroom in
Italy. Angela Campochiaro, the woman who had had her
hair cut while in a Potenza cinema with her fiancé, told the
jury via the court-to-court, international link, 'At first I
thought he [Restivo] had his knee against my hair and that
it was caught … I turned around two or three times. He had

his jacket over his lap and one hand underneath it. He then got up and left.' Later, she spotted him sitting behind three younger girls.

The couple have since married and her husband, Nicola Marino, demanded of Restivo what he was doing, but did not get an answer. It was as he confronted Restivo that he noticed to his horror that Restivo was masturbating. But it was not until the following day that Ms Campochiaro realised that her hair had been cut.

In cross-examination, Mr Jeremy suggested to Mr Marino that he had 'assumed' Restivo had been masturbating.

The witness replied emphatically, 'I didn't conclude it. I saw it.'

Elisa's brother, Gildo, gave his evidence from the witness-box at Winchester Crown Court. He said that Restivo had been very pushy about taking Elisa for a walk and he had come between them, telling Restivo to go away. On the day Elisa vanished, she had left home at about 11.20am with her friend, Eliana, to attend Mass at the Most Holy Trinity Church. 'That was the last time I saw my sister,' he said.

He added, 'I had a funny feeling, a strange sensation. I knew Elisa too well and what Eliana had relayed to me didn't convince me properly.' Eliana had explained that, as they exited the church, they lost sight of one another.

After pressing Eliana further, she confessed that they had not attended Mass. 'Elisa had an arrangement with Danilo Restivo to meet him behind the church,' he said. Eliana had seen Elisa walking towards the church, but 'from that moment she hadn't seen any more of her. When I heard the name Danilo Restivo my anxiety increased even further.' Gildo phoned Restivo, who sounded 'very agitated'.

Giovanni Motta, who, in 1993, was the boyfriend of Restivo's sister, Anna, saw Restivo walking towards his parents' home just after 1.00pm on Sunday, 12 September. 'He seemed fairly agitated and asked for us to take him straight away to the hospital because he had an injury,' he said.

Paolo Santarsiere outlined her meeting with Restivo a week after Elisa's disappearance. In answer to a question from Mr Bowes, she alleged, 'He said if anyone made him angry, he was capable of brutal actions.'

Speaking in fluent English from the witness box in Winchester, Italian pathologist Professor Francesco Introna, chair of legal medicine at the University of Bari, gave evidence of his examination of Elisa's remains after she had been found in the church.

Some of the injuries had been inflicted by a knife, but others were more likely to have been caused by scissors, he said. To help the jury, he deployed a ruler to demonstrate just how the incisions had been made in Elisa's body. A picture of a skeleton was also produced in court to help the jury to follow the grouping pattern of the wounds. Twelve of the punctures came from stabbing, but another was a cut, probably the result of Elisa struggling in an attempt to save her life.

The professor said, 'The different angles of the wounds showed that she either moved or tried to escape or avoid the rapid, successive blows.'

Prof Introna was confident that Elisa's attacker had been behind her the whole time. The trail of wounds was from 'back to front'. However, three of the stabs had been into the front of Elisa, with the attacker reaching round from behind, something that was scientifically provable. He agreed with Mr Bowes that the violence could have been sexually motivated. Elisa's knickers had been partially lowered, her bra unhooked at the rear and broken at the front, between the cups. Bruising around the pubic region, thighs and breasts also suggested a frenzied, sexual assault. Light-brown hair beside the body had been 'perfectly and squarely cut'. This had been most likely done while the strands of hair were stuck together by Elisa's blood, he said. Then the body had been covered with tiles.

Another Italian medical professor, Cristina Cattaneo, had found two single strands of hair, about two centimetres long, in both Elisa's hands during the postmortem examination. She believed that the hair scattered around Elisa's body in the loft of the church had been cut with scissors.

Dr Eva Sacchi told the court that Elisa's trousers were undone and unbuttoned. With the help of graphic photographs, she demonstrated where Elisa's knickers had been cut with scissors and her sweater had been hoisted to the region of her shoulder blades. Scissors had also been used to snap the bra, she said.

Yet another Italian witness was Colonel Giampietro Lago, of the Italian Carabinieri. He told the court that a jumper Elisa had been wearing was DNA-rich with both male and female traces, to such an extent that the source could only have been from body fluids and not skin flakes. Semen had been discounted, which meant that the deposits were either blood or saliva. 'In my experience, given all the circumstances, it is most likely to have been blood,' he said. 'I am highly confident of that.'

Forensic team-leader Claire Stangoe admitted that

saliva could not be ruled out, although blood was also a plausible explanation.

In robust cross-examination, Mr Jeremy said, 'To cut to the chase, you cannot exclude the possibility that the DNA came from blood, saliva or skin flakes?'

'We absolutely cannot rule anything out,' she conceded. 'This is an extremely complex case.' She further explained that she did not have the expertise, or indeed the testing procedures at her disposal, to go any further than the report she had already presented to the court, which had its limitations.

One revelation that was clearly earmarked for any post-trial soul-searching was the fact that there was some conflict between the CPS and the police as far back as 2004, when Restivo was arrested on suspicion of murder. Detectives on the case were opposed to releasing Restivo because they feared he was a danger to women and there could be more murders. However, because, at that stage, almost all the evidence against Restivo was circumstantial, the CPS feared that a jury might give him the benefit of any doubt, and he would walk. From then on, the surveillance operation was stepped up significantly. Not only was his home bugged, but also his car. For months, running into years, he was followed everywhere he went. His house was continuously watched during the day, but not always at night, when police officers were often needed elsewhere to deal with emergencies.

The real drama came at the start of the fifth week when Restivo took the stand. There had been much speculation over whether he would give evidence and therefore expose himself to a lengthy, sustained grilling by the prosecution in cross-examination. A defendant is not obliged to take the risk of incriminating himself, but either way it is a gamble. If a man is pleading not guilty, the jury likes to hear him protest his innocence in person, in his own words and prove his honesty against all attempts by the prosecution to puncture his defence. Jurors are supposed not to be prejudiced against any defendant who opts to stay out of the witness box, but you cannot legislate over human nature.

So there was an almost tangible frisson in Court Number Two as Restivo walked confidently from the dock to the witness box. The dock is hidden from the upstairs gallery, so this was the first time that the public had a view of the accused. Once again, as he had been throughout the trial, he was smartly dressed in a pinstripe suit.

Restivo made no attempt to deny his hair-cutting fetish, which he said began in Italy as a bet with other teenagers at his school when he was about 15. After he had tried it the first time, he got a taste for it. Speaking in Italian through his interpreter at his side, he said, 'The first three times was a bet between schoolmates. I was about 15 and I wanted to be accepted into the group. Then I started liking it. I meant no harm to anyone. I just like the feel of the hair and the smell of it.' But he strenuously denied that there was any sexual stimulus or satisfaction derived from his fetish. 'I did not realise cutting someone's hair would be an offence,' he added. 'If it was, I apologise.'

The atmosphere was electric as, head held high, he stared fixedly at the jury across the bowl of the court and declared, 'I have never killed anybody.'

Restivo's counsel, Mr Jeremy, focused on the day of Heather Barnett's murder and the moment he hugged her children. 'You know the prosecution case is that that morning you murdered their mother. It is also their case that by comforting the children you were playing out a repulsive charade.'

Restivo replied, 'No, it was sincere.'

Explaining his relationship with Heather, Restivo said that he had only met her the week prior to her death to ask her to make curtains for his wife's bedroom. 'I gave Heather a green towel which was the same colour I want,' he said. When quizzed by Mr Jeremy about where he had got the towel, he answered, 'I don't remember.'

Mr Jeremy said, 'In one interview you said you didn't remember giving a towel to Heather Barnett. In another you said you gave one of several towels to her. These are two different explanations. You see the difference? Both can't be true.'

Restivo claimed he was having memory problems and that he did not trust the police. And when questioned about why he had cleaned his trainers with bleach shortly after the murder, he said that he thought he was using soap; he had had no idea it was bleach.

On the issue of hair found in a Tesco carrier-bag in his bedroom, he believed that it might have been planted there by someone who had broken in on behalf of the Claps family.

One taped conversation concerned the cutting of a girl's hair in Bournemouth while she was on the way to school. 'I suffered sleep apnoea at the time and I could not remember things, like why I went to the fridge, for instance,' Restivo said.

'We are not talking about going to the fridge, we are talking about creeping up behind a girl and cutting her hair,' Mr Jeremy reminded his client. 'Are you saying you can't remember?'

'Yes,' Restivo replied.

Restivo admitted that he had declared his love for Elisa Claps in July 1993, but she had rejected him. He said that he had met Elisa in church on the day she disappeared to discuss with her his relationship with another girl. Despite evidence to the contrary from other witnesses, he maintained that he was not familiar with the church and was unaware that it had a loft. Elisa had left the church without him, while he stayed to pray, he said.

When he eventually exited the church, he walked to a nearby building site, where new escalators were being constructed, attracted out of curiosity because of the ingenious design. And it was there that he tripped, falling into mud and cutting his hand on sheet metal. He had used his denim jacket to help stop the bleeding.

Mr Jeremy wanted to know why he had refused to answer questions from Italian prosecutors about Elisa's disappearance.

Restivo replied, 'I felt they were fishing for someone to blame.'

He went on to claim that he had been physically and mentally abused while in solitary confinement in prison on remand.

Earlier in the trial, the prosecution had told the jury about the surveillance on Restivo while he was in the countryside at Throop Mill, near Bournemouth. The knife in his possession had been found, he insisted, saying, 'There were children playing nearby so I picked it up. I tried to show police where I found it, but they weren't interested.' He was in the country to relax and enjoy wildlife, not to stalk women. The balaclava in his car was there for wearing on cold mornings because he had a sinus condition.

Also earlier in the trial, CCTV footage had been shown of a man, identified as Restivo, heading towards Heather Barnett's address on the morning of the murder, but he was adamant: 'It was not me.'

Returning to earlier evidence, Mr Bowes said to Restivo, 'On 19 May last year, you were confronted with a towel that had your DNA on it and you said you have never seen it before. Overnight you decided to come up with a better story.'

On the following day, 20 May, Restivo claimed to the police that he had given Heather Barnett the green towel as a colour match for curtains he was ordering for Fiamma. This was before the couple married, but were living together. For several years before 20 May 2010, in interviews and witness statements, Restivo had denied all knowledge of the towel.

Continuing, Mr Bowes said, 'I suggest you never gave Heather Barnett a towel and that the reason your DNA was on it was that you wiped your face on it, after you killed her.' The prosecutor contended that talk of buying curtains from Heather was a 'pretence', solely for the purpose of planning her murder. 'I suggest you went back the following week, went into her lounge and killed her, didn't you?'

'No, don't insinuate things that are not true,' Restivo retorted, clearly irritated. 'I won't accept that. I was at NACRO all that day.'

Mr Bowes then concentrated on alleged 'inconsistencies' in Restivo's statements. On oath, Restivo had sworn that he had only gone as far as the hallway of Heather's flat when visiting her to discuss curtains. Yet, in a witness statement six days after the murder, he claimed to have gone into the lounge, where Heather showed him a catalogue of curtains.

'You must have known the layout of the lounge, you must have been there some time,' said Mr Bowes.

Restivo made no comment.

'Both Elisa Claps and Heather Barnett had their hair cut after they were murdered,' Mr Bowes went on. 'Do you agree that is a similar feature?'

'I don't know.'

'And do you agree that both having their bra cut and their trousers lowered is a similar feature?'

'I haven't killed either of them.'

'Does it look like the killer of both victims liked cutting hair?'

'I don't know,' Restivo replied.

Giving a reason for bleaching the Nike trainers he had been wearing on the day of Heather's murder, Restivo said, 'I did it because Fiamma told me they smelled and I did not know it was bleach. I thought it was soap for cleaning the floor. Up to last year, until I received the paperwork for the case, I did not know that bleach destroys DNA. I am not a forensics expert.'

Mr Bowes retorted, 'I suggest you are lying and that you bleached them to get rid of any contamination from the murder scene.'

Restivo repeatedly told the jury that he was at his computer at NACRO at the time of the Bournemouth murder. He also denied Mr Bowes's accusation that he kept locks of girls' hair as trophies and had taken one such 'trophy' to squeeze into Heather's hand after killing her.

During the next day of the trial, Thursday, 23 June, Mr Bowes revealed to the court that the police had seized a brand new set of knives, in a box, from Restivo's address. The knives were identical to the one discovered in his possession at Throop Mill, where Restivo claimed to have found the knife while watching wildlife.

Mr Bowes stated, 'They were pretty much identical to the one found at Throop. You went out and replaced the set because it was your knife all along.'

Restivo replied, 'My wife went out and bought a new set because the knives we had were not sharp enough. The fact they are similar, that's simply a coincidence.' He added that when he came across the knife at Throop Mill, his inclination was to make an emergency call to the police, because there were children in the vicinity, but his mobile phone was in his car.

B: You are just making up a story about the knife, the little children and the emergency. It is just fantasy.
R: No.
B: What you were doing all along with the knife and tissues and balaclava and gloves was stalking women, weren't you?
R: No, no, no. I was there simply to relax, to enjoy nature, and I was collecting and picking up insects. I have never stalked women.
B: Except on buses?
R: On the bus, that was not stalking. I was just on the bus without stalking them. I didn't follow anybody at Throop.

Explaining his movements on the morning of the murder, Restivo said he had been working on and off the Internet at

NACRO between 9.15am and 10.15am, before realising that he had not signed the register.

> R: I automatically looked at my watch and put down 10.30am, and then I deleted and wrote 9.00am, which was the actual time I arrived.
> B: What you have done, you actually arrived at 10.10am.
> R: No.
> B: Then later you go back and alter it to try and support your false alibi.
> R: No, I arrived at 9.00am.
> B: So up to now we have three versions. Version one, "I arrived at 9.00am and worked on the computer." Version two, when you heard the expert evidence and said, "Oh, perhaps someone else was using the computer." And after you have been served with the forensic report from Craig Wilson you made up version three, "I had the password all along."
> R: I have always had the password.
> B: Well, that's for the jury to judge.
> [Restivo was given the opportunity to read the evidence of the computer expert.]
> B: There was no user activity between 9.30am and 10.00am, and 10.00am and 10.10am.
> R: Yes.
> [Mr Bowes rolled his eyes and shook his head. He then switched to the murder of Elisa Claps.]
> B: You attacked her and stabbed her, didn't you?
> R: I saw Elisa leaving the church.
> B: She struggled back, didn't she?
> R: I saw Elisa Claps leaving the church at 11.50am.

[Restivo was shown a photo of the loft in the church where Elisa's body was unearthed.]
B: That's the loft where you took Elisa?
R: I've never taken anybody there. I didn't know it existed. I saw Elisa leaving from the church.
[Mr Bowes accused Restivo of using 'bait' to lure Elisa to the church to meet him, by saying he had a gift for her.]
R: I never mentioned presents to Elisa or anybody else. I don't know where this idea of a present has come from.

Restivo had exploited a similar ruse years later when lying to Heather Barnett that he wanted to buy curtains from her, when in reality he planned to kill her, said Mr Bowes.

Restivo replied, 'I have never killed anybody.'

Dr Denise Sydercombe-Court, called by the defence, disagreed with prosecution DNA expert Col Giampietro Lago over his conclusion in relation to stains on Elisa Claps's jumper. Col Lago believed that the male DNA residue on the clothing was most likely blood, rather than saliva.

Mr Jeremy said to Dr Sydercombe-Court, a specialist in DNA analysis, 'Col Lago said he thought it was more likely from blood. What do you think?'

She replied, 'I don't believe that I could come to the conclusion. I couldn't say whether it is blood or any other fluid-rich DNA.'

The doctor explained to the jury that there were numerous reasons for a test to 'flag up a false positive', including enzymes released during decomposition. She conceded that it would be 'difficult' for saliva to be deposited deliberately on the rear of a jumper.

In cross-examination, Mr Bowes asked the doctor if she was

suggesting that the opinions of the other expert witnesses were 'unreasonable'.

Dr Sydercombe-Court replied, 'He's [Col Lago] come to conclusions based on extensive experience but might not have looked at this. I cannot decide whether this material is from blood or saliva. I have considered the various tests. I have considered their reliability in the field and they are good tests. I am unaware of how they will fall in such a situation.

'I have looked at the literature and I can't see anything that will guide me, other than other scientific work that supports the fact that these tests go wrong and I would prefer to disregard it.'

Mr Bowes asserted, 'Well, you said they're not worthless.'

'They're worth something in standard forensic work,' Dr Sydercombe-Court said. 'I'm not sure they're worth anything regarding the age of the body in this case.'

Mr Bowes observed, 'There's a difference of opinion between you and Col Lago.'

These exchanges concluded the case for the defence, bringing the trial to the end of the fifth week. Before the court adjourned for the weekend, the judge told the jury that closing speeches by Mr Bowes and Mr Jeremy would be heard on the following Monday and he would sum up on the Tuesday.

After so many years, the end-game surrounding the murder of Heather Barnett was about to be played out.

-19-

THE UNMASKING
OF A KILLER

In his final speech, Mr Bowes said that although the jury had been bombarded with a barrage of scientific evidence from 'just about every forensic technique that exists, in the end this is a very straightforward case. Danilo Restivo is the man who killed Heather Barnett.

'You may think the defendant was evasive in the extreme and suffered from selective memory loss. There were some things he simply could not remember and others that he would remember very clearly.'

Restivo, he said, had 'stalked and selected and preyed', in both England and Italy, to feed his fetish for surreptitiously cutting women's hair in public places. 'The same person killed both women and that was the defendant. There were not two random killers.'

Restivo's explanations relating to the two murders 'ranged from the absolutely absurd to the ridiculous,' he argued. And Restivo's behaviour at Throop Mill in 2004, when under police surveillance as he allegedly spied on women, while in possession of a knife and scissors, was 'thoroughly sinister, whether he was reliving or rehearsing.'

By 2002, nine years after Elisa's death, Restivo was lusting to kill again. Forensically aware, all his criminal deeds were methodically planned, said Mr Bowes. 'The defendant's approach all along when questioned is that either he can't remember, or he lies, or he comes up with a ridiculous explanation. He has told lie after lie, but his lies have found him out. There is a reason that all the evidence points to him – it is because it is him.'

Mr Jeremy conceded that his client was 'a liar and a deeply unattractive oddity', but that did not make him a killer.

The police had Restivo fingered as the perpetrator years ago and, from then on, according to Mr Jeremy, 'it was just a matter of amassing the evidence over time'. But this was a dangerous game, he warned. 'That is the danger of collecting the evidence to fit a theory of guilt.'

Because Restivo had lived most of his adult life as a murder suspect – firstly for the Elisa Claps killing and then for the mutilation of Heather Barnett – this could explain his paranoia complex and 'victim status', he reasoned. 'This is a highly unusual case in which a defendant is charged with the murder of one person but the jury hears evidence of a second murder,' he said.

The jury had laughed at Restivo when he gave evidence and Mr Jeremy agreed that their mockery was understandable because he had 'self-destructed'. 'The jury might come to the conclusion that there was something childlike in Restivo's conduct, blaming illness for many of his problems and telling lies, often changing his story and exchanging one lie for an even worse one.'

Mr Jeremy accused his opposite number, Mr Bowes, of over-elaborating the evidence. He urged the jury to err on the side of caution, especially DNA evidence recovered from the green towel in Heather Barnett's flat.

'You have heard no evidence of violence in his [Restivo's] history that comes close to identifying him as a murderer. You will make a human judgement of him from his time in the witness box. If you are sure it is him, then you have promised to convict. If you are less than sure, then you have promised to acquit.'

Having a hair-cutting fetish did not make Restivo a killer, he stressed.

In his summing up, the judge, Mr Justice Burnett, told the jury that the evidence relating to Elisa Claps's murder was relevant to the Heather Barnett crime. The cutting of hair and bras, and the unzipping of trousers and the placement of the victims' hands amounted to a 'signature or hallmark of the killer,' he said. 'Both bodies had been arranged in a strikingly similar way.' Cutting people's hair against their wishes was certainly a crime of assault.

Reminding the jurors of their duty, the judge said it was their decision – and theirs alone – to decide which evidence to accept and what to reject.

Restivo's marathon stay in the witness box spanned four days 'and he failed to focus on questions asked of him,' said the judge. 'His answers were contradictory and even preposterous, something acknowledged by Mr Jeremy [Restivo's own counsel]. But he implored the jurors not to 'throw up their hands in horror and to reject out of hand' Restivo's defence. Many of the witnesses, including Restivo, were trying to recall events of many years ago.

'Murder, mutilation and children coming home to find their mother that way are bound to generate strong feelings, but you must leave emotion aside and make a dispassionate assessment,' said the judge. 'You are not bound to accept the arguments of counsels, but you mustn't speculate.' He underscored the importance of never forgetting that the burden of proof rested with the prosecution. 'The defence has to prove nothing. The prosecution must make you sure. If they don't, then you must acquit.'

For a guilty verdict, the jury had to be confident that 'three elements' had been substantiated: (1) that Restivo was the perpetrator; (2) he was acting unlawfully; (3) at the time, he intended to kill or cause serious bodily harm.

To kill lawfully, the perpetrator would have needed to be acting in self-defence, which, said the judge, could be excluded because of the ferocity of the crime and the obvious intent to kill. 'The only issue to be considered is whether it was the defendant who killed,' he said.

Much of the evidence was circumstantial, which, said the judge, 'can be powerful but needs careful examination.' There was DNA evidence to incriminate Restivo, particularly on the green towel. The bloodstained trainers were within the size-range known to have been worn by the killer, who almost certainly changed his clothes before leaving Heather Barnett's flat. Restivo was caught changing clothes at Throop Mill, while in possession of a knife very similar to the one used to mutilate Heather. Computer experts demonstrated that Restivo was not at the NACRO centre when he claimed to have been – crucial to his alibi.

If the eye-witness Claire George could be believed, Restivo was seen approaching Capstone Road at 9.20am, just before Heather was murdered, when Restivo insisted he was a few miles away on his NACRO course.

There was a striking similarity between the two murders, with both bodies arranged identically. There was no disputing that Restivo's DNA was on Elisa's clothing, but there was a dispute between expert forensic witnesses whether it was saliva or blood. Whichever, the defence maintained that it had been deposited innocently and not while a crime was being perpetrated.

Although convicted in Italy for perjury over Elisa's murder, in a trial that lasted a month, Restivo claimed that he had been wrongfully convicted.

'The prosecution says to believe Restivo's account of his involvement with Elisa on the day she disappeared, she would have to have left the church after meeting Restivo, only to return to the same church a few minutes later with another man, without being seen outside by the people waiting for her.

'It is also the prosecution case that nine years and 1,000 miles are connected by the hair-cutting fetish. You are entitled to consider all the evidence surrounding both murders. If you look at the whole of the evidence, the only conclusion must be that one person committed both crimes. Was it the defendant or some other person?'

The judge ruled that if the jurors were not certain that Restivo had killed Elisa Claps, then they should disregard all of that evidence and concentrate only on the Heather

Barnett issue. This would entail even discounting Restivo's conviction in Italy.

'Being a proven liar did not automatically mean that Restivo was also lying when he declared that he was not a murderer,' said the judge. 'People lie for different reasons — sometimes to try to emphasise their innocence or perhaps to save themselves from embarrassment. There are also many reasons why a person presents a false alibi. But if there is fabrication without an innocent explanation, then it supports the prosecution case. But a lie can be told to avoid the shame of disgraceful behaviour.'

Mr Justice Burnett advised the jury to apply 'special caution' when evaluating evidence of identification, referring specifically to the CCTV footage that appeared to show Restivo approaching the vicinity of Heather Barnett's home on the morning of the murder. The footage did not reveal the man's face and witness Claire George made the positive ID merely from the man's walk and mannerisms. Mrs George had seen Restivo many times in the chemist shop where she worked in Charminster Road, Bournemouth. The judge appealed to the jury to bear in mind the grainy quality of the film. The clip was short and disjointed, and the witness had seen it only once, when it was shown on the *Crimewatch* programme. 'Honest witnesses have been known to be mistaken,' he cautioned.

However, he did say, 'You may think the defendant lies when it suits him or to fit a story.'

The summing up lasted more than five hours and it was just before 11.00am on the Wednesday of the seventh week that the jurors were finally sent out to consider their verdict.

Five hours later, just before 4.00pm, the jury returned a

unanimous 'guilty' verdict to an eerily hushed courtroom, where emotions seemed to have been contained and were only released minutes later outside, where the mood was more of relief than of vengeful triumph. Leaving the court huddled together, bonded in grief that had miraculously strengthened them for so many years, rather than weakening them, members of Heather's family sobbed silently. Daughter Caitlin had been there every day of the trial, saying afterwards, 'I had to be there for my mum. That day when we came home to such horror has changed me for ever. It's hard for me to trust people. I was never like this before. My mum was a wonderful, trusting, laughing, friendly person.'

As the verdict was read out, Restivo remained as implacable as he had done from the beginning, standing like a statue.

The judge, maintaining the imperturbable serenity and quiet dignity that he had brought to the trial from day one, quietly thanked the jury for 'the care' they had taken and told the jurors that they would be welcome to return the following morning to see and hear sentence being passed.

Outside the court, Supt Mark Cooper said, 'The conviction of Danilo Restivo comes at the end of a very complex and challenging investigation for Dorset Police that was continuous over an eight-and-a-half-year period. The 12 November 2002 was a very dark day for many people following the brutal murder of Heather Barnett, not least for her family and particularly her children.

'This was a truly horrendous and distressing murder that took away a person who was very special to so many people. When he took Heather Barnett's life, he took a large part of many other lives.

'I believe that this dangerous predator had watched

over Heather for some time and carefully planned this horrendous crime.

'Despite his guilt, Restivo never moved away from his house that looked out on to Heather's property and, perhaps most chilling of all, he even consoled her two children that afternoon following his cold and calculated actions.'

Dorset's Crown Prosecutor, Alastair Nisbet, said, 'The Crown Prosecution Service would like to thank the witnesses who came to the court to give evidence in the course of the trial, including other women whose hair Danilo Restivo had cut without consent, and other members of the public and expert scientific witnesses.

'Our thoughts are with Heather's children and her wider family. I hope that this conviction brings some small measure of comfort.'

Heather's sister, Denise Le Voir, paid her tribute:

Over the eight long years waiting for someone to be charged with Heather's murder, our greatest fear was that the killer would murder someone else. It is now obvious that Dorset Police shared that concern and we are grateful to the many officers who carefully monitored Restivo's whereabouts and activity, hour after tedious hour to keep women and young girls in the Bournemouth area safe.

As new tests became available, they were used and new research flowed from the work. We are grateful to the many forensic scientists who have helped to solve the case, including all the backroom staff whose careful work on thousands of tests was represented by the experts who gave evidence in court. And I praise the jurors for having seen through the tissue of self-serving lies from Danilo Restivo.

Heather loved her children very much. She would have been horrified at the cruel and callous way Danilo Restivo designed her murder and mutilation so that her children had to find her body on return from school. She was kind and honest with strong ethical principles which she passed on to her children, Terry and Caitlin. She always worked very hard at whatever she did and built up a business on word of mouth and reputation.

Heather was feisty, had a deep laugh and a wicked sense of humour. Right from the start of the investigation, we were warned by the police that the killer was forensically aware and it was going to take more than Agatha Christie to sole this mystery.

The years since November 2002 have been difficult. But it has also been a time that has brought out the best in countless people, strangers and friends alike. We see ourselves as survivors, not victims, of Danilo Restivo and look forward to continuing our lives safe in the knowledge that this man will be kept away from the public for many years.

Heather was known to her friends as 'Bunny'. Her father, Denis, a wartime pilot Squadron Leader, sported a large handlebar moustache, a trademark of fighter pilots in those Battle-of-Britain days. Heather was musical and sang in her church choir, often performing solos. The whole family was popular locally because Heather, sister Denise and brothers Jeremy and Ben took part in local pantomimes, with mother Janet cast as principal boy.

A lover of animals, which probably explained her many excursions into the countryside, Heather briefly worked in a veterinary surgery and then in southern France as an au pair. Her one unfulfilled ambition had been to visit New York and see a hit musical on Broadway. But on her return from France, she worked variously as a waitress and in a jeweller's shop before retraining as a seamstress, which had always been her forte.

During the investigation, the police collected more than 700 statements, 6,200 exhibits and 7,300 documents. During much of the time, the case leader was Det Supt Phil James, until his retirement in 2007, when he was succeeded by his deputy, Mark Cooper. Supt James, like Caitlin, was in court every day. 'The pressure is always there in a case like this and you can't help but become emotionally involved because of the circumstances, particularly what was done to Heather and the fact that the children found her,' he said. 'Even when I retired, it is still with you.'

His main concern was that Restivo would strike again because James believed that he was a serial killer in the making. 'It meant at times we had to have him under surveillance 24 hours a day and we had to ensure we had him under control,' he said after the trial.

Supt James also revealed that he had warned Restivo's wife several times that she was in danger. After that, she 'pretty much made sure he did not go out alone, which made our job a bit easier.' Restivo kept applying for jobs at hospitals in the south of England and the police had to keep intervening, warning of the risks. Eventually, Restivo found employment as a dental technician.

During the trial, there were several telling moments outside the court. After concluding his opening address to the jury, Mr Bowes went into a huddle with his team and police officers and said, rubbing his hands, 'The jury are locked into this. They are focussed. They get it.' And just before Mr Jeremy went into court to start the case for the defence, he muttered to a trainee barrister, 'You will never see a day in court like this again.'

One of the public misunderstandings during the long and complex investigation was why it took until 2008 for the skin-flakes from the green towel in Heather's flat to be matched to Restivo's DNA with a 57,000:1 chance of an error. Repeated forensic tests had been conducted on the towel, but it was not until 2008 that forensic scientists had the technique to make the discovery. This was one of the innovative breakthroughs which had been alluded to by Denise Le Voir.

Italian TV journalist Pierangelo Maurizio had been a close observer of the Restivo case right from the day Elisa Claps disappeared. 'You have to understand the capacity of Danilo Restivo for lying,' he said. 'He's so quiet, so inoffensive, but a criminal who is very able, very clever, very careful. He takes the view that he can kill and then play a game with the police – catch me if you can.'

The brother of Elisa Claps said, 'In Italy, there were so many things that didn't work,' he claimed. 'The courts didn't investigate Elisa's disappearance properly. There are so many people responsible.

'I have fought because I could not allow injustice. I hated him and I still hate him. Elisa is the last thing we think about before going to sleep and the first thing we think about in the morning. She was a very sweet girl, quite sensitive and maybe she trusted people too much and this is something we always told her not to do.

'I wanted to stop Restivo harassing her but she didn't

want me to because she had sympathy for him. He couldn't find friends.'

Restivo was charged with Elisa's murder and is due to be extradited to Italy for preliminary court hearings in November 2011. But whatever the outcome in Italy, the deal was for him to be returned to the UK to serve his sentence for Heather's murder, although at a later date an agreement might be reached for him to serve his time in a prison in his homeland.

Before passing sentence on the morning following the trial, Mr Bowes read this statement from Caitlin:

Words cannot really say what happened on 12 November 2002. I screamed out and Terry called 999. He said mum was dead but I could not take it in. My heart had been ripped out and it was months before I could accept she was dead.

We lived in a hotel for a while and then with friends and family, including Denise. I love my brother dearly and he took the role of my protector. My school was wonderful and they tried to help.

I want to be known for who I am, not the daughter of a murder victim. What happened forced me to grow up more quickly.

I will never get the chance to say I love her [Heather] or how I miss her. My home has been taken away and I've never been back.

I have chosen not to be a victim. I want my mum to be proud of me and Terry. If I had the power I would lock him [Restivo] away for the rest of his life. I came to court to see justice done.

The judge told Restivo that the evidence of guilt had been 'overwhelming'. He continued, 'The evidence proves without doubt that you murdered Elisa Claps as well. I approach the sentencing as if you have killed before. You went to Heather's house to kill her and mutilate her. You cut her throat. You had a change of clothing to minimise forensic contamination.

'You arranged the body in a very similar way to that of Elisa Claps. You cut Heather's hair and left it, just like Elisa.

'There is no doubt that your motivation was in part sexual. You set up an alibi in advance. Your alibi was demolished by the weight of evidence.

'You knew two children would find the butchered body of their mother. "Inhuman depravity" is an apt description. You are a cold, depraved and calculating killer. You unleashed destructive forces on the whole family.'

And the judge's final words to Restivo are an appropriate conclusion to this extraordinary but truly chilling insight into the darkest side of human nature: 'In my judgement, there is no minimum term to be set. You will never be released. Take him down.'

As Mr Jeremy had said to his trainee, 'You will never see a day like this in court again.'